press play

press play

Patti Gordon

Multnomah® Publishers *Sisters, Oregon*

PRESS PLAY
published by Multnomah Publishers, Inc.

© 2006 by Patricia A. Gordon
International Standard Book Number: 1-59052-487-X

Cover design by Brand Navigation

Unless otherwise indicated, Scripture quotations are from:
New American Standard Bible
© 1960, 1977 by the Lockman Foundation
Other Scripture quotations are from:
The Holy Bible, King James Version (KJV)
Holy Bible, New Living Translation (NLT)
© 1996. Used by permission of Tyndale House Publishers, Inc.
All rights reserved.

Multnomah is a trademark of Multnomah Publishers, Inc.,
and is registered in the U.S. Patent and Trademark Office.
The colophon is a trademark of Multnomah Publishers, Inc.

Printed in the United States of America

For information:
MULTNOMAH PUBLISHERS, INC. • 601 N. LARCH ST. • SISTERS, OR 97759

Library of Congress Cataloging-in-Publication Data
Gordon, Patti.
Press play / by Patti Gordon.
p. cm.
Includes bibliographical references (p.   ).
ISBN 1-59052-487-X
1. Gordon, Patti. 2. Christian biography.   I. Title.
BR1725.G642A3 2006
277.3'083092--dc22
[B]
                                                      2005036816

06 07 08 09 10—10 9 8 7 6 5 4 3 2 1 0

To Mom and Dad:
the other great teachers of my life.

Contents

Section 4: Finding the Lover of Your Soul

thank you...

▶ When God gives us an assignment, He always blesses us with exactly what we need to accomplish it. Paramount in the blessings God provided as I worked on getting this book into your hands were people to help and support me along the journey. We all have our limitations and weaknesses, and God knew just who I would need to shore up mine. Many are old friends I have known for years. Others are new friends I met in the process of writing. But old or new, each played a crucial role in bringing this book to fruition. I will treasure each in my heart for many years to come.

First, I would like to thank Lorraine Pintus, a talented author, speaker, and friend who was by my side from the very beginning. She saw something promising in the first few pages I sent her. From that point on, she was always there asking the same wonderful question: "What can I do to help you?" Despite her own frantic schedule of writing, speaking, and taking care of a husband and family, she reviewed chapters, shared her incredible insights, helped me brainstorm, prayed with me, and listened to me cry. Thank you, Lorraine. So much of this book is a tribute to you. I will always be grateful for your generous heart and years of precious friendship.

I would also like to thank Donna Moody, another gifted writer and friend who has made priceless contributions to my life and to this book. Donna met with me on many mornings over a cup of coffee and a glowing computer screen, looking for that elusive "something" that makes a chapter work. Her sensitivity, honesty, remarkable writing ability, and treasured friendship have been such an encouragement to me, not only during the process of writing, but also throughout the years I have known her. Donna has always been there for me—even though I am sure it has cost her countless hours of sleep.

Penny Whipps is a gift from God. I have no doubt that God set up the strange set of circumstances that brought Penny into my life. In the middle of it all, Penny introduced me to Multnomah. She encouraged, supported, and made me laugh like no one but Penny could. I praise God for my wonderful, wacky friend with a precious heart for God and one of the greatest talents for promotions and PR that I have ever seen.

I also want to thank David Sanford, a literary agent par excellence with a passion for God and people. After an amazing whirlwind of events, I ended up standing dumbfounded with a book contract in my hands. I didn't know a thing about publishing and didn't have a literary agent, so David volunteered to review my contract for me. He made sure all the i's were dotted and t's were crossed. Then he wouldn't let me pay him. I am honored to know a man who demonstrates, in so many ways, that his life is all about glorifying God.

Dorit Radandt Dacre is a precious friend and one of the sweetest people I know. Dorit opened up the world of publishing for me. Many thanks, Dorit, for all you have done to bring this book to fruition. But the greatest gift you have given me is your steadfast love and acceptance through the years. You have seen me at my very best and at my very worst. Thank you for loving me anyway.

Jennifer Barrow is a talented editor with the patience of Job. Her insight into what each chapter needed was uncanny. I would beat my head against the wall for weeks trying to figure out what was wrong with a section; then Jennifer would make one simple suggestion, and the whole page would light up. (How do you do that, Jennifer?) In any event, many thanks, Jennifer, for your wonderful insights, your sweet friendship, and all of your hard work.

There are many more people I need to thank, but there simply aren't enough pages. So many friends and family members have prayed for me, encouraged me, given me their honest feedback, and stood by me through thick and thin. I have learned much about love from their lives. Thank you all for every word of encouragement, every prayer, and every time you told me you loved me. You are an integral part of each line in this book, and I thank and praise our awesome God for you.

Patti

foreword

▶ Oswald Chambers said that "the author who benefits you most is not the one who tells you something you did not know before, but the one who gives expression to the truth that has been dumbly struggling in you for utterance."[1]

Before you dive into the first chapter, I want you to know: You are going to love this book. And you are going to fall in love with Patti as you read, *not* because she tells you something new, but because she poignantly captures in words the elusive rumblings of your soul, the fears and dreams of your own life.

As you read, you will laugh (oh my gosh, the humiliation of her first class speech makes mine look like a piece of cake). You will cry (I could so relate to the agony Patti felt when she learned that not only her dad had been killed in a tragic accident, but her two sisters as well). Often you'll feel a sense of gratitude to Patti because as she seeks to follow God to the core of her being, she expresses the doubts you have feared to say out loud, doubts that are burningly honest: *God, I've prayed and prayed to You. Are You deaf? Why don't You answer my prayers?*

Sometimes the doubts Patti expresses are angry: *I know why this happened, God. YOU set me up!* Sometimes they are hopeful but uncertain: *Okay, God, this doesn't feel good, but I'll do it because You seem to be leading me in this direction.* But always the doubts are searingly honest: *Lord, how is it that You continue to deny me my dreams when I have followed You with every ounce of devotion I can muster?*

I know that this book will encourage you—that Patti's life will encourage you. How can I be so certain? Because I've known Patti for over thirty years, and so often she has been an encouragement to me.

I'll never forget the first day I met Patti. I was struck by her large doe eyes and gentle cooing voice. I sensed in her a strange mixture of velvet and steel. Several times I thought, *This girl is just too nice. She can't be for real.* But then I got to know Patti, *really* know her. I met her family. I saw her on good hair days and on days when she would say that a sheet over her head would have been an improvement. I listened to her dreams. I heard her anguish over deep losses and disappointments. I watched her walk through all kinds of circumstances, from the wildly weird to the mundane routines that entrap us all. And through it all, I witnessed firsthand the authentic way Patti lives her life and her relentless pursuit of God in spite of genuine doubts.

Patti is the real thing, and these days that is a rare commodity. I don't know about you, but I want to hear and learn from someone who is real. I don't have much use for mirages and theories that tickle the ears but don't stand up against the violent gales of real life.

There is one more thing I think you should know before you venture into these pages. Patti has a heart, a big one. And she cares about *you*. Oh, she may not know you by name or be able to describe your face, but she feels your longings, and her heartfelt prayer is for God to satisfy your deepest desires. I know because I have been with her, on my knees, and I've listened as she has cried out to God on your behalf, asking Him to touch you as you read and to speak to you in your present situation.

Patti's reason for writing this book has nothing to do with vain imaginings. Writing this book has cost her—*a lot*—but she knew her sacrifice would be worth it if in some small way God would touch you through her words. So go ahead. Turn the page. But first, may I say a prayer on your behalf? Because it is my desire as well to see God work in your life. And God's Word makes it clear that enjoying the good things of God begins with a simple request to ask Him to work (Matthew 7:7–8). So pray with me…

Lord, I don't believe it is an accident that I now hold this book in my hands. I believe that You have directed me to pick it up because You want to say something to me, to encourage me, to teach me. So right now I open my heart to You. I lay aside anything that would hinder me from hearing what You may want to express to me. Please, Lord, speak to me. I am listening…

Lorraine Pintus
Speaker and coauthor of *Intimate Issues* and *Gift-Wrapped by God*

how it all began

I was in my midthirties and had been fighting off a bad case of midlife crisis for about a year. I'd never married, had a job I didn't like, was broke, and in short, felt like a failure. All those dreams of a happy life with a man I loved seemed even more remote than they did back when I was sitting in Mr. Massey's algebra class stealing a peek at Jim Johnson to see if he was stealing a peek at me.

Ever since I was old enough to bat my eyes at the neighbor boy, I had prayed for a husband. Once I got a husband, life would fall in place. I would wrap my life around his, help with his ministry, make him happy, and spend his money. It was all quite simple.

But even though I showed up at what seemed to be every singles event the church sponsored, a ring never appeared on my finger and a man never appeared at my side. I was left counting the candles on the cake each year, wondering if I would be the one sitting in the nursing home watching all the other old people's children and grandchildren scurry by. Would I be the one huddled in the corner clutching the little green afghan given to me by some tender-hearted lady at Christmastime—the kind who asks the staff nurse, "Who can I cheer up that doesn't get many visitors?" Would I be the one they quietly whispered about as they tried not to stare? "She never married. What a pity."

Those were the places my mind would wander. Those were the days when I was miserable. No purpose, no future, no hope. Those were the days when I cried out to God and begged Him to change my life—to *do* something, by golly—to give me love, security, and peace.

And He did.

Oh, I got what I wanted. But it was not in the package I expected. I did not get a husband, a fat bank account, and a purpose—all on a silver platter. It was even better. I got love, security, and peace that did not rely on something that could change, die, or leave me. I got a hope that could go the distance.

And the package wasn't even delivered in a way I would have guessed. It came in a series of life lessons that only God could have engineered—lessons about the truth. This book is about those lessons and the new life they brought.

A life where everything was different—but the only thing that changed was me.

Patti Gordon

finding a
▶ family

Love always means going to others,
not demanding that they come to us.

PAUL TOURNIER, *ESCAPE FROM LONELINESS*

The bond that links your true family is not one of blood,
but of respect and joy in each other's life.
Rarely do members of one family grow up under the same roof.

RICHARD BACH, ILLUSIONS

1

the promise

▶ The engine coughed. Then quiet.

I was going to see Mark.

I pulled the key from the ignition and slipped it into my purse.

Powdery light from the street lamps sifted through the chilly night mist painting shimmering rings along the ribbon of asphalt. Iridescent puddles of rainwater danced on the pavement. The moon was full.

My shoes clicked a steady cadence that echoed along the car-lined street. I was running late, again. I had managed to get home from work at a fairly decent hour, but by the time I made dinner, breezed through the mail, and rifled through my closet for something appropriate to wear, I was running a good twenty to thirty minutes behind.

I wanted to see Mark. He would be there tonight, along with a host of friends and acquaintances—all with stories of days gone by, yet each with a new life fashioned from old fears, new loves, and persistent prayers. I longed to see them all again, but it was Mark who drew me there that cold and rainy evening.

It had been almost three years since a friend from church introduced me to this legend of a man. For months before I met him, I had heard wonderful things about Mark. From the moment I met him, I knew they were true.

Mark was a tall, dark-haired runner whose heart of kindness reflected in his gentle smile. The contentment of another world seemed to rest within him. He was at peace—totally, completely—with himself and with his world. Everyone I knew was drawn to Mark, young and old alike. Someone was always waiting to talk with him whenever I saw him at church or in a crowd. Waiting for that encouraging word that he so guilelessly gave.

Mark and I enjoyed mutual friends, chatted when we saw each other after church or at Bible study, and had a couple of hour-long conversations on the phone. I loved to talk with him. He was not the type to stay on the surface for long. He always listened, yet he always knew just when to share treasures from his own life. He challenged me to see the world from a different perspective and search through the clutter of life for the things that would last.

I was drawn to Mark, but something inside me kept him at arm's length. Several times he asked if we could get together. I longed to say yes and chat over dessert or a hot cup of coffee. Yet somehow I could not write his name on my calendar. I wanted to listen to him laugh as we fed ducks in the park down the street. But all I could hear was the echo of a promise I had made many years before.

I was fifteen years old. Summer rain pelted the sliding glass door. The creek swelled until it overflowed onto the grassy banks of our backyard. The thunder rolled. But we were safe and sound inside our beautiful Tennessee home. Mom sat in a kitchen chair. I stood behind her, my hands on her shoulders. Two of my sisters stood by our side. Dan and Carol Toner, our neighbors and dear family friends, stood before us. Slowly and haltingly they found the words. There had been an automobile accident. My father was dead. Two of my sisters were dead.

I stood—stunned.

This couldn't be right. Not them. Not us. Not me.

Yet their words continued, beating their awful truth into our lives. Suddenly. Fiercely. Unfairly. I wanted to run. Somewhere…anywhere…to a place where none of this had happened, where our front door would open and my sisters would bound through, where Dad would hold me tight and tell me they had lied.

But I couldn't run. There was no place to go. Instead, I stood behind that kitchen chair, numb, helpless, disbelieving.

For a while I thought I was strong enough to beat it, to never feel the pain of following three silent hearses as they wound their way past my father's childhood home. Yet as the numbness waned, the pain began to seep beneath the veneer of my smile. Longings stirred, and memories found their way into each moment.

But I had to fight.

I had to be strong.

I knew that if I let just one small drop of feeling slip into my hollow heart, a tidal wave of pain would follow, and I would surely drown.

Then no one could save me.

I had shared a room with Barbara. She was eleven when she died. I remember the first night I lay awake and stared across the moonlit room at her empty bed. It was neatly made; the pillow placed just so, just the way she always left it. She should have been

lying there, her silky blond hair falling across her forehead, the softness of her breathing gently reminding me that I was not alone. I
wanted her to know how sorry I was that I had fought with her the
last time I saw her. I wanted to tell her that I loved her and missed
her very much. I wanted to thank her for her unselfish willingness
to always let me have the last M&M.

Janet was ten when we buried her. She had tried so hard to be
my friend, but I so rarely found time for her. I would brush her
aside as I left to take a walk with a neighborhood friend or refuse
to play with her as I retreated to my room to read a book. I wished
that I could tell her how sorry I was for the tears I had caused. I
wished that I could let her know how much I really loved her. Now
I would give anything to help her with her homework, brush her
hair, or let her beat me at another game of Hearts. It was especially
hard to know that Janet would not be coming home.

Then there was Dad. *Oh Dad, how can I possibly face this world
without you?*

Two years later I finally cried. The pain broke through. Great
waves of sorrow pounded on my heart, and I did the only thing I
knew to survive.

I made the promise.

I'm not sure exactly when. It might have been on graduation
day. I longed to see Dad's beaming face peek from behind the cam-
era as I walked across the stage. I had studied hard for him. Or it
might have been on a Saturday night when I needed him to shake
hands with a boy I was dating and let him know he was expecting
me home by twelve. Or maybe it was when I missed his laughter
at Christmas or his arm around my shoulder at the Tri Delta parents day dinner. I don't remember exactly when, but I made a
decision, a promise if you will…

Never again will I let anyone so deep into my heart that they can hurt me this badly when they leave.

Across the street, another lone figure threaded its way along the sidewalk and through the row of cars parked like motionless soldiers guarding the building ahead. I stepped to the curb, looked both ways, then dashed across the street. Warm golden light streamed from the windows and beckoned me up the steps to the front door. No need to knock tonight.

Inside people were everywhere—one hundred, maybe two. Lots of warm embraces as old friends greeted each other for the first time in years, a steady hum of voices catching up to the present, telling tales of the past, remembering.

I plunged into the sea of faces and began my search. Where was Mark?

My eyes came to rest on an old roommate stationed contentedly with her new husband only a few feet away. I slipped in beside her to deliver a smile, a few words, a quick hug, then moved to the circle of another dear friend. And another…and another. Like wandering through the pages of an old, familiar book, I made my way through the crowd, immersed in the comfort and familiarity of people with whom I had shared so many chapters of life. Their voices stirred forgotten memories sweetened with the tempering of time. Yet another voice whispered softly from within, reminding me of unfinished business to which I must attend.

Where is Mark?

I inquired, then followed a pointed finger to a cluster of people standing by a wall. Of course. I should have known that Mark would be surrounded, as always, by people who loved him. As I gazed at the huddled group of his friends, my resolve weakened. I wasn't sure I was ready for this, but it wasn't my choice, or my timing, for that matter.

"Excuse me. Pardon me. Oh, I'm sorry, excuse me."

I reached the group and stood silently behind a solid wall of shoulders—faithful friends, side by side, oblivious to the swarming crowd behind them. I rose to my tiptoes, straining for a glimpse. A head turned, kind eyes met mine, and a step aside sent a ripple through the gathering as each surrendered a tiny space that made room for one more. As I stepped into the opening and found the countenance of my friend, a flood of emotion was pierced by a tiny ray of relief.

At least the casket was open.

Mark's face was peaceful, as always, but the cancer they had found just before I met him had taken its toll. His cheeks were hollow and pale. His thinning hair revealed a crooked scar—evidence of the many attempts this world had made to keep him. His eyes were closed in a final farewell to the pain that had etched his soul and then, in turn, touched the depths of ours.

The lines of his face softened as a watery veil appeared before my eyes. I stood, transfixed, silently gazing at what was no longer the Mark I knew. His voice was silent. His smile had disappeared. I stared at a shadow of what had been—an empty vessel with the indescribable privilege of having held, for a place and time, a truly remarkable soul.

I stood. I waited. I hoped against hope that the softness of his lashes would flutter open again to reveal eyes that could see through souls. I prayed. I remembered. Then I swallowed hard, reached up to brush the cool trickle from my cheek, and drank in one last memory of the friend I almost knew.

Turning, I silently made my way back through the crowd—lost in the darkness of a world of regret. I had known that Mark was dying when I met him. He had beckoned me in, but a promise to protect my heart had robbed me of a treasure.

I would never know the richness of hours across a table sharing stories of our childhoods. I would never feel the breathless joy of struggling to keep up with the long-legged runner as we raced across the grocery store parking lot. I would never hear him tell me all the lessons God had taught that helped him live and die so well.

He would never laugh with me until we cried. He would never taste my apple cobbler on a Sunday afternoon. He would never know the comfort of my hand in his as he struggled for his breath upon that hospital bed.

I turned the metal knob and stepped into the misty evening. The door clicked. The hum of voices ceased. The frosty world enveloped me—colder, emptier than it had been before my last good-bye.

The silence of the night was broken only by the staccato of my heels as they tapped their familiar rhythm along the street. The world drifted by, a sentinel of soft gray buildings shrouded in a dreamlike haze.

It was finished. Mark was gone. Yet his memory echoed through the emptiness of my life. For Mark was not the only one I had kept outside my world.

How many lonely evenings had I longed for someone who really knew me? How many tasteless meals had I eaten all alone? How many Sunday mornings had I watched them leave—two by two, three by three, family by family—while I stood smiling, bidding them farewell until another week passed and I would once again sit next to them, inches away yet worlds apart?

How many times had I looked away, out of fear of rejection, when a glance and a smile could have encouraged a soul or opened the door to a new world of friendship? How many times had I covered my feelings with quick wit and laughter, only to steal the precious honesty that binds heart to heart? How many times had I refused to feel the love that I was afraid I would lose?

I reached inside my purse and fumbled for my keys. Opening the door, I sank into a crumpled mass on the seat. Dejected, exhausted, longing for another chance to stand behind that kitchen chair and live my life, from that point on, so differently.

I now saw my promise as the traitor it was—a sepulcher of safety, a prison fashioned from my fear. I'd trusted it to keep my heart safe, but it had never sheltered me from pain. Pain had always found me. The only thing that promise had ever kept from me was love.

And love was all I had ever wanted.

I sat. I wept. I wondered.

Would I ever find a place of safety—a fortress from the misery that love would leave behind? Was I to spend my days without the hope of comfort…or healing…or peace?

Then, as if to answer, a still and quiet voice awakened in my heart and whispered, "Come to me, all who are weary and heavy-laden, and I will give you rest."

I raised my head.

I knew that voice. It was the voice of One I trusted. He understood my grief and sorrow. He Himself had born the cross of pain and died for me and rose again. And He had told me:

"I will not fail you or forsake you." (Joshua 1:5)

Such beautiful words. But were they true?

Where had He been those many nights when I lay crying, long-ing, praying for my family to be whole again? Where had He been those countless evenings when we sat down to dinner with three empty chairs? Where had He been those Christmases when no one could hang the lights quite like Dad?

Where was He now when all of life seemed hopeless?

Softly…gently…I sensed a stirring in my heart, a tender touch. Then I sensed His presence. I felt His peace that passes under-standing. It blanketed my soul and calmed my heart. Unexplainable. Undeniable. He was there, beckoning me. In His still and quiet voice, Jesus called to me that night…

And I came running.

His peace washed over me like waves upon a shore, and with it came a simple understanding that He had always been there, wait-ing, wanting me to turn to Him for comfort, longing to heal my broken heart. I knew that He was there and that He loved me.

I would never have to look upon His body in a casket. I would never hear His last good-bye. I would never have to weep without Him. He was my God and my bastion of safety. For I was His daughter, and He was the Father who would never leave.

Six years have passed since Mark's death, and God has proven faith-ful. He has become my rock, and from that rock I can reach out and risk rejection. God's perfect love gives me strength to open up my heart, for now I know that He can heal the pain that love might bring. Through His love He teaches me to love, and life has mean-ing.

I know I will see Mark again someday, face to face. We will talk and laugh, and I will thank him for the many ways he changed me.

I will tell him stories of fears I have surrendered and of love I have found. But most of all I'll thank him for that cold and rainy evening when, even in his silence, he proclaimed the truth. And in that truth I found a new beginning,

a new love,

and a broken promise.

"Come to Me, all who are weary and heavy-laden, and I will give you rest."

MATTHEW 11:28

2

there you are

He reached over and touched my face. His eyes met mine. We smiled.

The strains of a faraway love song wafted on the still night air. My gaze wandered through his ebony locks then dipped, again, into the deep pools of his brown eyes.

"Partly sunny with a low of thirty-eight and a high of forty-five degrees..."

I lifted my arm and groped for the little turquoise button that would give me ten more precious minutes of sleep. *It can't be eight o'clock already. There...*

His smile had slipped into a land of dreams, but another stole across my face as I remembered that his was real, and I would see it again today. I closed my eyes, nestled into the softness of my comforter, and pulled its warmth snugly around my neck.

Memories of the evening before drifted through my mind.

Richard... My head on his shoulder, his hand on the small of my back. Dancing across the polished wooden floor. His gentle yet confident movements flowed perfectly with the music and were so easy to follow. How could I have wondered what kind of dancer he would be? He was wonderful at everything he did. He was one of the most successful salesmen in his Fortune 100 company—quite an accomplishment for someone who was not yet thirty-five. He was a leader at church, very popular with the ladies at Sunday school, and had the most infectious laugh of anyone I knew.

I had been surprised to hear his voice on the telephone—making small talk, laughing a little, then asking me to his company's Christmas dinner and dance. I had admired him from afar for a very long time. Of course, the answer was yes.

It was a storybook evening. I stepped into the pages when he offered his arm and escorted me from coworker to coworker. His eyes smiled as he playfully fed me another olive (he promised I would love them if I ate three). Then he held my hands in both of his, looked into my eyes, and asked me for the honor of a dance. There was no doubt. My Romeo had finally arrived.

It was close to 1:00 A.M. by the time he walked me to my door. I asked him in, and we sat on the sofa chatting for what seemed a few minutes—but the clock on the mantel told us an hour had passed. We stood up, he kissed me softly on my cheek, and the cold air whispered across my face as the door swished open and closed.

"...*in a one-horse open sleigh.... Jingle bells, jingle bells...*"

That obnoxious alarm clock! But this time I didn't have the luxury of ten more minutes filled with visions of Richard. Sunday school started in an hour. Maybe I could see him before class if I hurried.

My feet hit the floor, and within minutes the bathwater was running. I plugged in my electric curlers and dashed out to the kitchen for a quick bowl of Wheaties. Was he thinking of me too?

Maybe he would ask me to lunch. I couldn't wait to tell Donna how he introduced me to several of his friends as the "woman of his dreams."

I stepped into my closet and reached for the teal dress I had picked up on sale at Lord and Taylor. This one was a classic, great with my brown eyes. But wait. I got so many more compliments from men when I wore the black sweater dress. I had a feeling Richard would like that one better.

I rushed to the mirror. *Why won't my hair cooperate today of all days? Where's that brush? This lipstick's not quite right. Maybe a little more red.* I couldn't wait to see Richard again. A spray of perfume and one last look in the mirror. The earrings were perfect; the lipstick was just the right shade. I grabbed my keys and was off.

The drive to church seemed to take forever. I finally pulled into the parking lot and found a spot not far from the door of the singles Sunday school building. One last peek in the rearview mirror. Lipstick, blush, mascara—all fine.

Play it cool, Patti.

A man sauntered across the parking lot making his way from the early service. Was it Richard?

No.

I darted a glance at the street and found a few stragglers who had caught the tail end of the light. His six-foot frame and confident gait were nowhere to be seen. Maybe he was already inside.

When I opened the heavy wooden doors, I was greeted by the buzz of over two hundred singles. Women dressed to the nines. Men in coats and ties. Some were milling about looking for an old friend or a potential date. Others clustered in tiny groups—safe havens from the potential rejection of someone who might mistake a friendly smile for a desperate come-on.

I scanned the crowd. There he was, chatting with a group of his friends. *I wonder if he's been looking for me.*

Ten minutes until the main assembly began. Donna was not far from where he was standing. Surely if I got that close, he would see me and come over to say hello. *What will I talk about?* My heart fluttered. I'd think of something.

"Hi, Donna!" I greeted my friend with a hug. "How was your week?"

"Well, hi, Patti!" she replied. "It was busy! I went Christmas shopping every night, but I still haven't found anything for…"

I tried so hard to concentrate on her words, but my thoughts kept floating back to Richard. Would he ask me to spend the afternoon with him? Maybe he would ask me out for Friday night. We had talked about a movie we both wanted to see.

"How was your date with Richard?" Donna asked.

"Oh…" My mind snapped to attention. "Oh, Donna, I had a blast. He's an incredible guy! I'll have to tell you all about it."

I could see him out of the corner of my eye. He was laughing and joking—always the entertainer! Now it was only five minutes until main assembly. He must not have seen me yet. Maybe I should just go over and say hi.

Excusing myself from Donna, I squeezed through the crowd. Richard's voice got clearer and clearer. He was talking about his Saturday-morning basketball game. Stepping into his circle of friends, I caught his eye and smiled.

No response.

His story continued. Thirty seconds. It seemed like an eternity. Forty-five seconds. I glanced at the clock on the wall just over his shoulder. This was torture.

No hi. Nothing. No acknowledgment that I was even there. I

wondered if I should turn and leave or just melt into the floor. *Keep smiling, Patti. Act like you're paying attention.*

He finished. It must have been funny because his friends erupted in a hearty laugh. Then Bill, one of Richard's basketball buddies, turned to me, "Hi, Patti."

"Hi, Patti," others echoed.

There. Richard said it too. I tried to muster a happy-go-lucky smile and groped through the gray matter for something clever to say.

Silence.

Thank heavens someone started up the conversation again. I stood there speechless as my heart sank into my patent leather pumps.

Without a word, Richard turned his back and walked toward a beautiful redhead standing by the coffeepot. My feet were frozen to the spot for what seemed an eternity as I attempted to make conversation with the girl standing next to me. Finally I excused myself, pasted on a smile, and tried to look like I had somewhere to go as I stepped into the faceless crowd.

Tears sprang to my eyes. I could not let them fall. Not here.

What did I do wrong last night? Did I act too interested? Did I say something that offended him? Or was I simply a bore, and he was kind enough to act interested and attentive for the evening? Maybe he didn't like my hair or my dress, or maybe he thought I was too fat, or…

"Patti!"

A familiar voice jolted me back to the present. I lifted my eyes, and there in front of me was Jeff Morrison, arms outstretched, waiting to give me a big "Jeff" hug. His smile beamed like the flashlight of a rescuer breaking through to a victim who had been buried alive. I will never forget his voice, his smile, his hug that day. Jeff and I had been friends for almost three years, but in that split second, he nailed himself a permanent place in my heart.

A genuine smile stole across my face as I closed in for one of the sweetest hugs I can ever remember.

What a roller coaster ride that Sunday morning turned out to be. But when the sick feeling of that ride was over, it ended up being one of the biggest blessings of my life. That was not the day I learned how much rejection hurts—I had figured that out long ago. That was the morning I realized how much a hug can heal.

At a Christian conference I had attended years earlier, Joyce Landorf told us, "There are two kinds of people in this world: those that walk into a room and say 'Here I am' and those that walk into a room and say 'There you are.'"

I had heard it back then. I finally got it that morning.

The Apostle Paul wrote about it two thousand years ago in his letter to the Philippians. He said, "Do nothing from selfishness or empty conceit, but with humility of mind regard one another as more important than yourselves; do not merely look out for your own personal interests, but also for the interests of others" (2:3–4). I had memorized those verses years ago, but they had never found a home in my heart until Jeff Morrison became Philippians 2, with skin on, for me.

That Sunday morning, I began to pray that I would become a real-life Philippians "there you are" person too. I asked God to help me be the comfort to others that Jeff had been to me. Then I did my very best to focus on someone else. Sometimes I succeeded. Sometimes I failed. But before long I noticed a surprising phenomenon. Whenever I focused on other people, I ended up getting much more than I gave.

I got more smiles from people who were glad to see me than I ever could have imagined. People sought me out in a crowd, opened up their hearts to me, and told me I was an answer to their prayers. But the most amazing thing was the joy I felt when I went to sleep at night because I'd made a difference in someone else's day.

One of my greatest fears in life has been to end up lonely and unloved. But now I know that if I'm a "there you are" person, I will always have a friend, I will always have a reason to smile, and I'll never be without someone to care for and someone to care for me.

So thank you, Jeff Morrison, for being my friend and for being a "there you are" kind of guy. And, Richard, I thank God for you too. For even in my dreams I never imagined the love I would find because of you.

Do nothing from selfishness or empty conceit,
but with humility of mind regard one another
as more important than yourselves;
do not merely look out for your own personal interests,
but also for the interests of others.

PHILIPPIANS 2:3–4

3

eyes to see

▶ "Delta flight 1023 to Atlanta will now begin boarding at gate 20."

This was it. We'd heard these words many times before. We both knew what to do.

"Thanks so much, Mom. It was a wonderful visit." I leaned over to hug the sweet salt-and-pepper-haired seventy-five-year-old woman sitting next to me. As we sat back, she enfolded her soft hands around mine.

Mom was still beautiful—a surprising blend of polyester pants, sensible shoes, elegantly high cheekbones, perfect skin, and enchanting brown eyes. Her gracious manner was more befitting a Bostonian blue-blood than a sweet country girl from a farm in Nebraska. But a sweet country girl she was, with simple tastes and simple expectations.

But life hadn't always been kind to her. "We're survivors" became her proud declaration as our family weathered storm after storm. She had given six daughters to the world. Today she sat beside me a widow with only four. "If there is one thing I want to teach you," she had told me as we stood before three flower-laden coffins, "it's how to take it when times get rough." And take it she did—with a resilient spirit and an incredible determination to raise her remaining four girls to the best of her ability, to make something good out of our lives.

"Patti, thank you for coming for Christmas," she said as she squeezed my hands. "We love to have you home."

And I loved to be home for the holidays.

It had been a bustling week overflowing with warmth and togetherness. Mom, my three sisters and their families, and I had all crowded into her modest three-bedroom home.

Our days began in bathrobes around the kitchen table—Mom and her girls, nibbling cinnamon toast, sipping coffee, and chatting about last-minute shopping and what time to start the turkey. As the world awoke, husbands and children appeared at the doorway and began to wander into the kitchen. With sleepy eyes and growling stomachs, they stepped onto the green linoleum and ushered in the excitement of the day.

Stirring large pots of bubbling oatmeal. Refereeing skirmishes between sobbing toddlers. Running to the store for another gallon of milk. Shuffling a never-ending stream of dishes in and out of the dishwasher. Frosting Christmas cookies. Sweeping up colored sugar sprinkled on the floor by little hands not yet old enough to know the convenience of agility. Taking last-minute trips to crowded shopping malls. And wrapping gifts at midnight while Mom looked for more tape and an extra pair of scissors.

Then, like a four-measure rest in a frantic winter's symphony, the Christmas Eve fire was lit, Kathy passed out songbooks, and Mike tuned his guitar. Marshmallows bobbed in mugs of steaming cocoa while Mom piled gingerbread cookies onto a Santa Claus plate. The joy and peace of Christmas calmed our hurried hearts as

"Silent Night," "Joy to the World," and other family favorites rang through the rafters.

Christmas Day brought chocolate-covered cherries, mounds of turkey and dressing, cranberry-stained tablecloths, and naps on the family room floor. Then as quickly as it had descended like a whirlwind in our lives, another Christmas disappeared into a yesterday.

Excitement vanished. The house grew quiet. My sisters and their families prepared to return home. One by one, we closed suitcases and buckled children into car seats. We gave hugs and goodbye kisses. Then doors slammed shut, windows rolled down, and arms reached out for a final farewell wave. Mom and I stood shivering in the driveway, straining for one last glimpse as each family disappeared around the corner at the end of the tree-lined drive.

I looked at Mom's pensive smile and the hint of sadness in her eyes. "I know it'll be awfully quiet for a while, Mom."

She reached over and grabbed my hand.

We turned and ambled back toward the house as the neighbor's Christmas lights, nestled in snow-laden branches, twinkled in perfect silence.

"Flight 1023 to Atlanta, now boarding rows 25 through 35."

I looked down at my boarding pass.

"That's me, Mom." I slid the black carry-on strap over my shoulder. "I'll give you a call when I get to Atlanta." My lips brushed her velvet cheek, and I gave her one last hug. "Love you."

Christmas was over.

I walked to the gate agent and presented my ticket.

My visit had been rich—full of the blessings of belonging. But as the walls of the Jetway closed around me, the contentment of the past few days echoed its farewell. Behind me was the love and warmth of family. Ahead, a plane full of strangers and a world of silent mornings.

The memories of that Christmas were precious and yet so cruel. They dared to seep into the forgotten places of my heart and gently stir the longings I had so carefully lulled to sleep: longings for a husband and a family of my own, someone to love, someone to care for, someone to care for me.

My bulging carry-on bag bumped against the seat backs as I walked down the aisle of the plane. Twenty-four. Twenty-five. There...27B. I sank into the seat, let the black strap fall from my shoulder, and strained to cram the bag into the empty space in front of my feet. The seat belt clicked as I leaned my head back and closed my eyes.

Memories of this Christmas carried me back to days gone by, days of starting life together. The same laughter, the same voices, the same hearts. Mom and Dad in the front seat of the station wagon—six little girls in pink pajamas in the back. Windows down. The flutter of blond and brown curls still damp with the cool water of an evening bath. The chatter of little voices anticipating a frosted root beer mug filled with ice-cold refreshment after a sweltering summer day. Then, before I knew how much I would miss them, our precious childhood days surrendered themselves to Saturday night dates, final exams, and sharing sweaters.

After a few years, God gave my sisters husbands, families, and worlds of their own—worlds I could only visit. But where did I belong?

"Here are our seats, honey."

I opened my eyes. A little gray-haired couple was standing in the aisle. He hoisted a bulging shopping bag into the overhead bin while she stood behind him, clutching her purse, waiting patiently.

I smiled and imagined her gazing at him as he placed the angel on top of the tree. How many times had they tiptoed down the stairs together on Christmas eve? How many bows had they tied on packages that would soon be unwrapped by tiny little fingers? How many turkeys had she pulled from the oven as wide-eyed children clamored for a bite?

He gave the shopping bag one last shove as it slid into its perch overhead. Then he stepped aside and held his bride's elbow as she shuffled into the window seat across the aisle from me. "Thank you, dear," she said. Her face shone as she looked up at him.

I leaned my head back and closed my eyes again. Another wave of loneliness swept over me. Who would open the gifts I wrapped when I was old and gray? For years I'd been praying that God would give me someone with whom I could share my life. *Lord, why have You left me to wander through this life all by myself? Why haven't You given me a husband? Is there something so wrong with me?*

The bustle of other passengers boarding the plane grew faint as I drifted off to sleep.

Three hours later I heaved my suitcase into the trunk of my car. Then I rifled through my billfold to find a dog-eared ticket for the parking lot. It was late—almost 10 P.M. But even though sleep tugged at my eyelids and I longed for the warmth of my bed, as I drove I dreaded walking back into my apartment. I knew all too well that the silence waited. The lock would click, the door would open, and it would be poised, ready to swallow anyone who ventured into its icy domain.

Thump. Thump. Thump.

My suitcase bumped each step as I dragged it up the stairs to my front door. I turned the knob and flipped a switch. The room appeared before me. It was just as I had left it—frozen in time—waiting for my return.

I could still see the soft indentation in the sofa pillow where I had stolen a few precious moments of rest the evening before I left. A curl of red ribbon cowered on the floor just under the coffee table—the only survivor of a last-minute gift-wrapping session.

My little Christmas tree stood patiently in a corner of the living room, yet only a shadow of its beauty remained. Around its base lay a halo of pine needles that, one by one, had surrendered their lives like the dying festivities. Many quiet days without a companion had left it tired and spent. I understood how it must feel.

One empty coffee cup in the sink. One teaspoon on the counter. Painful reminders of living alone.

I wheeled my suitcase into the bedroom, unzipped it, and began the search for my toothbrush and toiletries. Within minutes I would escape to the safety of my dreams and an office full of coworkers that waited on the other side of sleep.

But first I had a promise to keep. I had told Mom I would call to let her know I was home. But no… This wasn't home. I was back in the place where I lived. That was all.

As I reached for the phone, the flashing red light told me messages were waiting. I grabbed a pen and paper and pressed play.

Click. "Hey, Patti! It's Ellen." A familiar voice pierced my despair.

I had met Ellen ten years ago when I moved to Atlanta. She was a girl from South Georgia with a sense of humor as rich as her southern drawl.

"We just got back from Mom's. I wanted to see how your Christmas was," she said.

Several years before, I had been involved in a struggling start-up business that left me almost penniless. During that time Ellen, her husband Rick, and their little boy, Fritz, opened their home to me for six months—rent-free—until I could get back on my feet. Such precious friends to help me through those difficult days—it was a gift I could never repay.

Click. "Patti, it's Brian! Just wanted to make sure you made it home. Give me a call as soon as you get in—it doesn't matter how late!"

Brian was like a brother to me. We had met at Sunday school, but we were also neighbors. We dated for a while, but before long it was clear that we were meant to be good friends—a solid friendship, forged through laughter, tears, anger, and forgiveness.

One late night, Brian had called and in a pitifully weak voice told me he had food poisoning. Could I come over and help him? I pulled on a pair of sweats and ran to his front door. Instead of the handsome, self-confident man I knew, I was greeted by a ghost—hair disheveled, skin pasty white, so weak he could barely stand. I cleaned up the bathroom floor and held his head until it was over. I helped him into bed and then lay down on the sofa—just in case he needed me for another round.

A couple days later, I got his "food poisoning" too. Of course, he felt horrible about it, but he was there for me—chicken soup in hand. What a blessing to know that we had each other.

Click. "Hey Patti!"

It was the voice of another sweet friend. Tara and I had met on Saturday mornings for coffee for months before she married Steele. We poured out our hearts, shared our fears, and decided that since Tara was an only child and my own sisters were a thousand miles away, we would be sisters at heart. She prayed for me every morning and shared her loving parents with me. Tara, with her mom and dad, made me feel like family as they welcomed me into their hearts and homes.

A tear trickled down my cheek.

Donna's message was next—my precious friend with the listening heart. She always sought to understand and knew, in her kind and gentle way, how to help me see the truth. God had used Donna many times to remind me how much I was loved.

Then I heard Becky's voice. Becky was a nut—full of fun and laughter. Yet she was as deep as anyone I'd ever known. With a heart that beat for God, Becky was someone I was honored to call my friend.

More tears began to roll.

My prayers for someone to share my life with had not fallen on deaf ears. God had been listening—and He had been answering too. He'd given me someone to love, someone to care for, someone to care for me. He'd given me someone who would stand with me through laughter, sorrow, and pain. And finally, today was the day He gave me eyes to see that not all of my family shared the same name. But every one of us shared the same Father.

Even though I would still pray for a husband, God had given me all that I needed for now.

With a very full heart, I dried my eyes, picked up the telephone, and dialed that familiar number. It rang once, twice…

"Hello?" My mother's sweet voice rang through the line.

"Hi, Mom," I said. "I'm home."

And I meant it.

Now we have received, not the spirit of the world,
but the Spirit who is from God,
so that we might know the things freely given to us by God.
1 CORINTHIANS 2:12

finding a

▶purpose

for living

Joy comes from seeing the complete
fulfillment of the specific purpose
for which I was created and born again,
not from successfully doing something of my own choosing.

OSWALD CHAMBERS
MY UTMOST FOR HIS HIGHEST DAILY DEVOTIONAL

You will never set a goal so big or attempt a task so significant
that God does not have something far greater
that He could do in and through your life...
Until we have heard from God,
we cannot even imagine all that our lives could become
or all that God could accomplish through us.

HENRY T. BLACKABY AND RICHARD BLACKABY
EXPERIENCING GOD DAY-BY-DAY

"Though it tarries, wait for it..." (Habakkuk 2:3).
We cannot bring the vision to fulfillment through our own efforts,
but must live under its inspiration until it fulfills itself.
Waiting for a vision that "tarries"
is the true test of our faithfulness to God.

OSWALD CHAMBERS
MY UTMOST FOR HIS HIGHEST DAILY DEVOTIONAL

4

plan b

I took a deep breath…
Held it for a wishful moment…

Then the flames of the candles clung for dear life as a giant gust swept across pink roses and swirls of chocolate icing. One by one, each tiny blaze disappeared into a stream of smoke rising from the tip of a glowing thread.

I leaned back as a smattering of applause crackled through the dining room. Becky called out another "Happy birthday!" as Ellen planted a pile of plates on the table in front of me.

Thirty-four.

So many candles on that cake. So many wishes that hadn't come true. So many years since a homespun girl from Omaha had pressed the fifth floor button in the elevator of Sandoz Hall. Mom had been beside me, balancing a cardboard box. I stood next to the rocking chair I'd somehow twisted past the closing doors and into the tiny crowd of anxious faces. Of course, I'd need a comfortable chair for reading.

Back in the parking lot, a brown Pontiac waited, filled with everything else I imagined I'd need during my freshman year at college. Somewhere in those boxes was a heart-shaped cake pan, a sewing kit with an assortment of buttons, and a glass vase big enough for a dozen long-stemmed roses. I was confident it would all come in handy someday.

You see, I was a planner, and I was prepared. I knew exactly what I wanted to be when I grew up: married. The rest of the details didn't matter much to me. I had no idea what to study during four years of college, but I had three good reasons for being there. First, I wanted to find a husband. Second, I wanted to become an interesting person for my husband. Last but not least, I wanted to prepare myself to bring in a little extra income to supplement my husband's paycheck. My major would become clear in time. For now, I'd just make sure I had matching earrings for every sweater and all the laundry detergent two people could possibly use in a year.

Months passed, and the shelves in my dorm room gathered a collection of books and football paraphernalia. Florescent lights glowed into the nights while pink and yellow highlighters left colorful trails across textbook pages.

The hunt for a husband didn't go quite like I'd planned. Most of the men that asked me out during my freshman year were just too wild for me. I spent Friday and Saturday nights trimming bangs, fastening buttons, tying scarves—getting all of my sorority sisters ready for their dates before I settled down to an evening of studying alone in my room.

But my day would come. I knew it would. It was only a matter of time.

After two years, I had a first-rate GPA and had even chosen a major. For years, Mom and Dad had encouraged me to go into teaching so I could have summers off with my kids. I loved math and science, but Home Economics seemed like a much more practical major. As for marriage, I had two more years of college. Surely the right man would come along by then.

But men were hard to find by my junior year. There weren't a lot of them in Home Ec, and I lived with sixty women in the Tri Delta house. By the time I was a senior and student teaching rolled around, I was still spending Saturday evenings with a set of pastel highlighters and an oatmeal facial mask.

Student teaching was, well, different than I expected. I envisioned rows of solemn students deeply engrossed in my brilliant pontification on the proper handling of thawed ground beef. As it turned out, I couldn't keep discipline in the classroom to save my life. Someone was always wandering around the back of the room, shooting spit wads, or cracking jokes in the middle of class. To add insult to injury, on the last day of school one of the boys showed me his notebook, which was filled with little pencil marks. He had been keeping track of all the times I had said "You know."

That semester, the only one who learned much of anything was me—and all I learned was that I didn't want to be a high school teacher. After four years of hard work and a whole lot of tuition checks, I reached for my diploma, shook hands with the dean, and tried to figure out what else I could be when I grew up.

After graduation, I got a job with the university that paid enough for me to live with three other girls in an apartment with orange shag carpet and to drive a beat-up car with the vinyl roof rusted through. The car became known around those parts as "Flash." I became quite humble.

University employees could take classes for a dollar per credit hour, so going back to school seemed like a logical thing to do.

Counseling would be a wonderful area of study—I could meet all kinds of sensitive men in my classes, and what a great expertise for a wife and mother! Every woman needs to know how to help her husband change, plus every teenager needs a mom who can straighten them out and teach them how to listen.

But all that studying and holding down a full-time job didn't leave time to go out with the guys from class. Before long, I had finished the coursework and was locked and loaded, ready to begin an internship in marriage and family counseling. It was time to put all that knowledge to use and help some real-life people for a change.

It was also time for another bubble to pop.

The internship was excruciating. Hour after hour I listened to the most dismal, depressing stories imaginable from men who had lost their families, children who had been sexually abused, and wives whose husbands beat them. I had clients whose spouses were cheating, clients whose spouses had died, and one man whose wife had tried to murder him three times.

By the end of the internship, I was exhausted, emotionally spent, and completely out of Kleenex. I can hardly remember the route home from work. I cried most of the time I was on it. Those people needed help so badly, but I couldn't figure out how to restore their mental health without losing mine in the process. Apparently, I'd stumbled onto yet another profession that was not a fit for me.

After another graduation and more hard work than I cared to recall, I had no husband, no way to make a living, and I was driving a car named Flash.

Not exactly the life of my dreams.

The next eight years brought a string of jobs for which I was ill-suited and horribly underpaid. Eight solid years of frustration.

To complicate matters, since I was single, I had to make enough money to actually support myself. That little detail still presented a bit of a problem.

As I sat back and stared at thirty-four smoldering candles, somebody handed me a knife.

Donna reached across the dining room table and helped me pluck candles from the gooey confection. Then I sliced into the mound of chocolate and slid a piece onto a plate. I laughed and smiled, acting like I didn't have a care in the world while I tried desperately not to think about the future.

The party was wonderful—a much-needed diversion. But as I climbed into my car next to a pile of boxes and bags and a rainbow of ribbons, the joy of friends and laughter disappeared into the summer night like smoke from the candles' smoldering wicks. In its place burned a proverbial question, a relentless whisper:

What are you going to do with your life?

The question had haunted me since childhood. Back then, it was easy to ignore. I thought I knew the answer. But as time wore on and life did not unfold as I had expected, it became an irritating itch, a pebble in my shoe, a nagging nemesis that would not go away.

Another birthday only added fuel to the fire. It accentuated the fact that after thirty-four years I had nothing to show for my life— no husband, no family, no career. Not for lack of trying! In fact, I'd worked hard. I'd spent all my time and energy doing everything I could to be in the right place at the right time with the right education to catch the right man.

Unfortunately, he never showed up.

Plan A was a miserable failure. And I never had a Plan B! Other than marriage, I couldn't think of anything else I really wanted.

So what was I supposed to do? I'd already wasted thirty-four years. I didn't want to waste another minute. The only thing I knew for sure was that someday—sooner or later—I would stand before the Lord, and He would hold me accountable for what I had done with my life.

I didn't want to stand there empty-handed.

Another red light. My foot hit the brake, and a pile of boxes slid to the floor. I glanced at a stream of bath oil beads spilling from a bottle, then back at the red light—too tired to care.

If I wasn't supposed to be married and raise a family, why in the world was I here? If God had another plan for me, why wouldn't He give me a clue? Didn't He know that if He expected me to do it, I needed to know what it was? Hadn't He heard that "if you aim at nothing, you'll hit it every time"? The last thing I wanted was to end up looking back at a life that had missed the mark simply because there wasn't one.

Of course, I hadn't exactly batted a thousand with planning in the past. Even though I'd made all kinds of plans, none of them seemed to come to fruition. I either needed a lesson in implementation or a heavy dose of reality—something to stop my nasty habit of aiming at the moon and the stars. But now more than ever, I needed to aim at something. If God wasn't going to give me a goal, I'd better come up with one on my own.

First of all, I needed to make a living. Maybe I should go back to school in engineering, or law, or maybe get an MBA. But the thought of more studying made my stomach turn like a pig on a barbecue spit.

I shut off the engine and leaned over the seat to stare at a crowd of renegade bath oil beads. I sighed. They would just have to wait until tomorrow. I was too tired to round them up tonight.

What about the ministry? I could work at a church or maybe

even an orphanage. I'd be floating around poverty level for sure, but at least I'd be investing my life in something that would last.

Or maybe I should go into sales. Sales could be a lucrative career. I hated the thought of asking someone to buy something, but if I was going to be miserable, I might as well do it with money in the bank. Besides, I could have a beautiful home, a sporty-looking car, and support that orphanage and church as well.

Over and over, my mind twisted and turned along the same track it had traveled hundreds of times before. But nothing hit home. Nothing felt quite right. I never found an answer to that proverbial question that whined like a siren with an endless battery.

It was bound to drive me crazy if I let it.

I watched a tiny trail of toothpaste crawl across the brush. It should have been a wonderful day, but turning the page to another year was more than a bit of a downer.

Another drink of water, another glance in the mirror… another wrinkle.

Exhausted and bewildered, I slid between the sheets and uttered one more desperate plea.

Lord, I beg You… Tell me what to do with my life.

I reached over and switched off the light.

Red numbers glowed from the nightstand.

The vent exhaled a long, cool breeze across my face.

Cars swished by outside my window.

I stared into a deep, dark ceiling.

The air conditioner hummed its familiar monotone.

Finally, I sat up, turned on the light, and reached for the Bible tucked beneath my bed. Its gold edges and burgundy leather were well worn from many hours of probing through its wisdom. There had to be something in there for me tonight.

I rustled through the pages and paused at the book of Jeremiah. There, at the bottom, was a verse I had underscored, long ago, with a line of blue ink.

"For I know the plans that I have for you," declares the LORD, "plans for welfare and not for calamity to give you a future and a hope." (Jeremiah 29:11)

A future and a hope?

Thank goodness *Somebody* had hope for me because mine was running on the south side of empty. I was tired—tired of trying, tired of failing, tired of that hollow, empty feeling of a life without a purpose.

But if God had a future prepared just for me, how could I find it?

Then I heard a single word. Not with my ears, but clearly in my heart.

Obey.

So strange… It came from nowhere.

But what did obedience have to do with my dilemma? I needed a goal from God. I needed a vision. I needed something big to shoot for.

But that simple message still echoed in my heart.

Obey.

Could it be? Surely not… It couldn't be that easy.

Then, as if in reply to that proverbial question, an avalanche of verses tumbled through my mind.

We are His workmanship, created in Christ Jesus for good works, which God prepared beforehand so that we would walk in them. (Ephesians 2:10)

Watch the path of your feet, and all your ways will be established. (Proverbs 4:26)

The mind of man plans his way, but the LORD directs his steps. (Proverbs 16:9)

Even though I'd memorized these verses many years before, that night I saw them in a completely different light. I realized that they held the missing pieces of a puzzle, and the answer to my question came clearly into view.

God said that He had already prepared a path of good works for me—steps that would take me where He wanted me to go. He didn't tell me where those steps would lead or what was in the future. He simply told me to watch my feet—to do the good work He put before me today. Then He would direct my steps to the next good work tomorrow.

I gently closed my Bible and leaned my head back against the wall.

So the key to my future was the path of my feet, not the road out in the distance. I didn't need to see the big picture after all. God knew why He created me, and I could rest assured that His path would lead me to accomplish His purpose for my life—one step, one good work, at a time.

Best of all, I didn't have to search to find the next step. He had already given me plenty of direction.

He had told me to love Him and to love my neighbor. To do my best at whatever work He put in front of me. To trust Him, worship Him, pray to Him, and honor Him. He said that if I would wait for Him I'd never be ashamed. He told me to be humble, honest, and kind. He told me to be generous, patient, and forgiving.

And that was just the start.

The Bible in my lap was full of His instructions for my life. As I obeyed those instructions, He would make me into the woman He wanted me to be—a woman prepared for the next good work—the next step on His path. As I obeyed, He would lead me and guide me. He would open doors that no man could open and close doors that no man could close. He would accomplish His plans for me—plans for welfare and not for calamity—to give me a future and a hope.

As I sat in my bed in that silent room, I felt a strange sensation. Peace.

The truth of that answer had broken through my heart and poured rivers of tranquility into my weary soul. The haunting question was silent. I finally knew the answer. I finally knew exactly what to do with my life…

Obey.

I slipped my Bible back beneath the bed, reached for the light, and lay my head on the pillow. Then I murmured a prayer of thanks to God for all He had shown me.

Somewhere in a peaceful haze that hovers between waking and slumber I thought I heard a distant voice echoing in the future.

Well done, good and faithful servant.

Somewhere in that peaceful haze I smiled.

"For I know the plans that I have for you,"
declares the LORD, "plans for welfare and not for calamity
to give you a future and a hope."
JEREMIAH 29:11

the setup

▶ The hinges creaked behind me. I stepped into the morning sun and shivered as a springtime chill crept up the sleeves of my tattered gray sweatshirt.

Morning has always been my favorite time of day, but this one was particularly enchanting. The night before, while I was sleeping, a masterful brush had swept through the neighborhood, sprinkling drops of pastel hues and planting hopes of brighter days ahead. I scanned a sea of golden lawns dusted with new green blades and watched a robin hop across a freshly spaded flower bed. (Breakfast would surely rise to the occasion.) Then I drew a breath of crisp morning air, slipped my hands into ragged pockets, and marched down the front porch steps.

I loved my walks through that New Jersey neighborhood. Most hours were lost in headphones listening to Keith Green. Others bestowed a luxurious time to think through life and pray.

I slipped the headphones into my pocket. Today was a thinking kind of day as I pondered my career. By now I'd finished graduate school in counseling, had realized I was too tenderhearted to practice, and had started yet another search to discover what life held for me.

A flight attendant job made sense, while I sorted through some options. I could travel to cities like Singapore and Paris and stay in exotic five-star hotels. I could eat at fancy restaurants, meet fascinating people, and maybe even find a husband.

Yep, flying was surely the ticket.

But somehow reality didn't quite match my imagination. Instead of a life of luxury, I got a beeper on my belt, sore feet, and a bad case of sleep deprivation. Calls came in at midnight for 4:00 A.M. check-ins and trips that no one wanted, like red-eyes from L.A. I spent January layovers in Detroit, Thanksgivings on a plane full of strangers, and Christmases alone in a hotel.

Oh, I knew that my schedule would get better over time, but it was becoming awfully clear that I was an eight-to-five kind of girl, and flying would never be an eight-to-five kind of job. How in the world did I get such a knack for finding careers that weren't right for me?

I stepped to the curb, looked both ways, and then trekked across the street.

Years ago, I had promised God that I would "dwell in the land and cultivate faithfulness" (Psalm 37:3). But that verse was getting pretty old these days. I'd been trying to be faithful for an awfully long time. I knew if I took one day at a time, God would unfold His plan for me—but I wanted some hope and encouragement *right now*. I wanted something to look forward to. So then and there, in front of Mrs. Austin's gate, I begged God to tell me what He had in store for me.

I had no idea how He would let me know. Quite frankly, I wasn't expecting an answer. I knew the Bible had never promised that God would tell me the future. I also knew that the key to my future was walking in obedience today. But I was tired of waiting, and it couldn't hurt to ask, could it?

My shoestrings resumed their *tap, tap, tap*. I turned the corner and started to stroll down another stretch of gray sidewalk.

But as I walked I felt a growing sense of disappointment in myself. I knew in my heart that I needed to be content wherever God put me. I needed to trust Him with my life—to "dwell in the land and cultivate faithfulness." So I confessed:

God, I know I'm being impatient. You promised You'd accomplish Your purpose for my life if I'd just be faithful and obey. But it's hard to be content when life feels like it's standing still. So help me to be faithful, Lord. Help me to wait for You.

As I passed another little white house with empty window boxes, I remembered a verse I'd memorized long ago:

"For from days of old they have not heard or perceived by ear, nor has the eye seen a God besides You, who acts in behalf of the one who waits for Him." (Isaiah 64:4)

A smile crossed my lips. I had accepted Jesus Christ as my Lord and Savior at the beginning of my freshman year in college. Since that day, I'd spent hours and hours studying the Bible and memorizing verses. All that wisdom was turning out to be the most precious treasure I had. God always had a way of bringing a verse to mind, to comfort or encourage me just when I needed it most.

Lord, thank You for reminding me that You are at work even when I can't see what You're doing. I know that I need to wait on You, and I promise I'll really try to do it. You know what You want me to do with my life, and You'll tell me when You're good and ready.

At that moment, I heard a silent whisper.

I want you to write and speak about Me.

I stopped. *What was that?*

I didn't hear an audible voice, but I sensed the words clearly in my heart. It was such a tiny whisper. It must have been my imagination.

I shook my head and strolled on.

Jesus said, "My sheep hear My voice" (John 10:27). But that statement had always puzzled me. What did Jesus' voice sound like? So several years before, I began to pray and ask God to teach me.

Was that His voice? How could I be sure?

Were those silent words the answer to my prayer or just the sausage from this morning's breakfast talking? Could God be speaking, or was it the whisper of an overactive imagination? Was this the clue I'd asked for or the moan of a heart that was desperate for an answer?

Many times in the past I had begged God to answer me. Would I get that job? Would Bill ask me out? Would I marry Steve? I'd pray and think that I'd heard Him say yes, but then nothing would happen. Later I realized the yes I thought I'd heard was just my own desires getting mixed up with my impatience.

But this seemed different. It was almost like my conscience—a gentle prodding deep inside my soul. Plus, those words seemed oddly familiar. During my sophomore year in college, I'd "heard" the exact same thing and promptly dismissed it as a ridiculous idea. Who in the world would want to read anything I wrote? Besides, what were the chances of actually getting published? I could confidently declare that *that* would take a miracle. And life as a starving writer didn't sound like my cup of tea. So I tossed the thought aside those many years ago and decided to pursue something more sensible.

Yet on that chilly morning, I couldn't toss the thought aside quite so easily. Those words took root inside my heart and tugged like the north pole on a compass needle.

I had to admit: there was nothing I liked better than the idea of writing and speaking about God. My relationship with Him was the most important thing to me. I'd love to help others get to know Him too.

But there was one small problem.

I didn't know a thing about writing. In fact, I didn't even like it. I had never taken a writing class in college—papers for other classes had made life miserable enough. All I remembered about writing papers was the gruesome struggle of trying to choose a topic, followed by another gruesome struggle that usually lasted most of the night—trying to figure out what to say about the ridiculous topic I'd chosen.

Why would I want to do that again?

To make matters worse, the only grammar class I ever had was back in sixth grade. Gary Benton's spit wads and Don VanDoren's jokes kept me so distracted that I hardly learned a thing. I didn't know the difference between a gerund and a gender, and onomatopoeia sure sounded like Greek to me. Plus, I had no idea what I shouldn't end a sentence with.

Not exactly the makings of another Margaret Mitchell.

And that was just the beginning. Not only was I totally incapable of writing anything worth reading, but just the thought of speaking in public put a knot in my stomach and buckled my knees. I was petrified to even ask a question in Sunday school.

Okay. That cinched it. I must have been hallucinating. It was nothing more than a ridiculous idea.

Mrs. Whitmier's pampered dachshund waddled out to greet

me. I stopped, stooped down, and scratched behind his velvet ears.

But think of all those people who are searching for the Lord....

Wow! This little guy is as big around as he is tall. What kind of puppy chow...?

But how can you be sure that those words weren't from God?

I stood upright and closed my eyes.

Let's see, I've got to remember to pick up the dry cleaning. Then I'll stop at the post office and head to the...

You'll never find a better way to invest your life.

I was losing this argument fast.

I opened my eyes and started walking.

Besides, you told God you would obey Him.

I slipped my headphones on and pressed play. But even the blaring strains of Keith Green couldn't drown out the next round.

For the gifts and the calling of God are irrevocable. (Romans 11:29)

Faithful is He who calls you, and He also will bring it to pass. (1 Thessalonians 5:24)

Checkmate.

I pressed stop. The silence was deafening.

Okay, Lord. I don't see how this could be from You. The only way I'll ever know for sure is if it happens. But if it's going to happen, You're going to have to do it because I sure don't know how.

I figured I was pretty safe. It sounded impossible to me. So I got a little braver.

If this is from You, go ahead and count me in. I'll go along for the ride. If You give me a chance to write, I'll give it my best shot. If You give me a chance to speak in public, I'll prepare what I'm going to say and open my mouth, but You'll have to take it from there. So here's my promise, pure and simple—if You open the doors, I'll walk through them.

That was easy enough.

I turned down my own brick walkway. Then I shoved that promise to the back of my mind and marched up the front porch steps.

A few months later I transferred to Atlanta. After two more years at the beck and call of a beeper, I got an eight-to-five as an administrative assistant for a land developer. It wasn't exactly the job of my dreams, but at least I knew what city I was in when I woke up every morning. Then something strange began to happen. My boss started asking me to write. At first it was just a few letters, then a marketing brochure. Before long I was writing investor proposals for land development projects.

But I sure wasn't having any fun.

After a couple of years, I moved to another company to manage corporate training workshops. The pay was better, and besides, how much writing would a training manager have to do? Yet my new boss asked me to write all kinds of things—letters, proposals, even a section of a book. But the real surprise came when I actually began to enjoy it.

After all those years, I started to get the hang of writing. The struggle to find just the right words began to feel more like a game. My sixth-grade grammar book was still in Mom's basement. So I pulled it out, cracked the thing open, and finally started to read. But what I liked most about writing was the sense of accomplishment I had when I was done. I didn't mind working hard for that feeling. In fact, the more I wrote, the more I craved it.

Then one day a friend asked if I would consider quitting my job to take a six-month writing contract with one of his clients.

Wow! A real company wanted me to write for them. It sure looked like an open door to me. Even though I wouldn't be writing about God, I would still be putting words on paper. That was a step in the right direction—or so it seemed. What an opportunity! The chance of a lifetime to step into a freelance writing career.

But it didn't take long to get my head out of the clouds and my feet back on the ground. I wasn't quite ready to give up a regular paycheck and the security of a full-time job. I had visions of rummaging though reeking trash cans and living in a box in some alley.

But I'd made a promise to God, and it looked like He was cashing in. Yet before I stepped out into the thin air of self-employment, I had another little talk with Him.

Lord, I'll give this everything I've got, but I ask one thing in return—that You provide the money for me to live. I know You want me to meet my commitments and pay my bills on time. So if You don't provide the money and a bill is ever late, I'll assume that You're not leading…and I'll stop.

The first six months were a piece of cake. The contract was for forty hours a week, and the pay was pretty good. But I pinched every penny, knowing it would take a while to build my clientele after the contract was over. I had a strange suspicion that things just might get rough.

They did.

Before long, I realized that there's nothing more depressing than another Monday morning without a billable hour in sight. Time and again, I reminded myself, "Faithful is He who calls you, and He also will bring it to pass" (1 Thessalonians 5:24).

If this whole writing thing really was from God, He would make it happen.

Sure enough, one by one, projects trickled in. And slowly, I added clients to my list. Between projects, I worked as a temp in administrative jobs. They took time away from writing, but they helped keep money in the bank.

And money in the bank was the name of the game.

On rare occasions when I went out to eat with a friend, I had only coffee for breakfast or a cup of soup for lunch or dinner. My kitchen cupboards held only the cheapest brands, and my closet hadn't seen a price tag attached to anything in ages. I cut my own hair, re-dyed my old black jeans, and prayed that I'd make it to the next gas station.

Oh, I lived on the edge—that was for sure. But it was only for a season. God would provide. After all, that was His part of the bargain.

With a little help from savings, I managed to pay the bills each month. But all good things must come to an end. My savings account was no exception.

I'll never forget the afternoon I withdrew my last dollar bill from that account. As I turned and walked away from the cold marble counter, I had the distinct feeling that I was plummeting headfirst off the high dive—only to realize that someone had just drained water from the pool.

Four weeks later, I hit rock bottom.

• • •

Click.

An eternity of silence.

Then the detestable drone of a dial tone.

I put the receiver back on the table and winced as I scratched a crooked line through the last name on my list. It had been a long, hard month of searching, and I hadn't found a thing. Every lead had fallen through. Every promise had been empty. Every path that I had sprinted down had only wasted time. A final round of calls to clients and no one needed the help of a desperate writer. Even worse, I couldn't find a temporary job opening in town.

Rent was due in three short days, and I had nothing—absolutely nothing—in the till. Worse yet, my faith was beginning to waiver.

Why wasn't God providing? Why in the world would He stop me now? I was finally learning some tricks of the trade. I was finally excited about writing for Him. Plus, what about all those open doors? That sense of peace? Those small successes along the way? Had I been mistaken to believe that He was leading? Had I been His faithful child, or had I been a fool?

The jury was still out.

But He was the One who had gotten me into this. He had called me to write, opened the doors, and then dried up all my savings. He had lured me out onto a limb, slashed the safety net, and left me dangling. He *had* to catch me. He *had* to come through. Didn't He?

I reminded myself again, "Faithful is He who calls you, and He also will bring it to pass" (1 Thessalonians 5:24).

Surely there must be work somewhere. Surely I could find it.

But I had already called every client and taken the typing test at every temp agency in town. I'd talked to everyone I knew at church, but no one was aware of a single company that needed help right now.

Don't stop moving, Patti. Don't give up. Just be strong and do something.

But my heart was heavy, my body tired, and try as I might, all I could do was sit on the sofa and stare.

Some time later, I dragged myself up and wandered into the kitchen. Maybe a cup of coffee would help. Maybe it would give me a pick-me-up and help me think of some new ideas. I spilled out the dregs from the last brew and opened the cupboard to grab the coffee can.

But where was it?

Oh, I'd almost forgotten. I'd finished it off this morning. I had decided not to get any more on my last trip to the grocery store. After all, $5.95 was an awful lot of money, and I needed things like milk and bread. Maybe I could do without coffee for a while.

I stood with my hand on the cupboard door and stared at the empty space on the shelf. *God...You even took my coffee.* I swallowed hard. My heart sank to my stomach. My chin trembled, and a tear ran down my face.

Don't do it, Patti. Don't give up.

But I wasn't very convincing.

Finally, I heard them—heaving sobs echoed through the kitchen as tiny rivers streamed down my cheeks. Face in my hands, I sank to the kitchen floor and sat there for a long, long time— helpless, hopeless, knees to my chest, back against the cupboard, sobbing until there were no tears left to cry.

Then I waited...for anything.

Shadows crept across the walls. The room turned gray. I mustered my strength to stand, stumbled to the sofa, and sank into the cushions.

Oh God, what kind of mess am I in? I could see it now: all my worldly possessions piled up on the curb, waiting to be hauled away by anyone with room in the trunk. How had it come to this? How had I ended up in this big game of chicken? *God, I worked so hard. How could I have lost so badly?* Unfortunately, the answer was becoming awfully clear. For quite a while now, I'd sensed it. Maybe it was finally time to admit it.

I had been betrayed.

Yes, God had set me up. He'd lured me into the middle of the ocean, then hammered a hole in the bottom of my boat. He'd pretended to open doors while I used up all my savings. When my bank account was empty and my little boat was sinking, He had grabbed the oars and jerked them away just to watch me drown.

And all I'd done was try to obey Him.

I sat and thought and cried…and sat and thought and cried some more. Then I heard a silent whisper.

I will not fail you or forsake you. (Joshua 1:5)

I struggled to sit upright.

Oh God, You don't understand. Don't You remember the deal? I would keep writing if You'd pay the bills. In three more days rent will be late, and I don't have the money for it—much less the late fee. Plus, next month's rent will be due before I know it.

No answer.

Then it dawned on me. Maybe it wasn't God's fault, after all. Maybe the fault was all mine. He never actually agreed to the deal.

Maybe I'd just deluded myself and concocted those words to find hope for my future. Maybe it was just a coincidence that all those doors to write seemed to open. Maybe the whole thing was just a crazy fluke—a deceiving set of circumstances that looked so promising.

I leaned back again and rested my head on a soft sofa cushion.

Maybe I'd never know what happened, but one thing I knew for sure. *It was over.*

After almost a year of pecking at the computer, racking my brain until midnight to come up with clever ideas, and searching for quarters under sofa cushions to buy a frozen yogurt cone, it was time to surrender my writing career.

I had failed miserably…again.

But now what?

I closed my eyes and watched splashes of light dance across the curtains of my eyelids. Deep inside I knew that shutting out the world wouldn't change a thing. But you couldn't blame a girl for trying.

I jerked upright and groped blindly in the direction of a ringing telephone.

I fought to find my senses.

"Hello?" I tried to sound coherent.

"Patti? Patti Gordon? This is David Schiff."

David… Bits of data spun through my sleepy mind like lemons in a slot machine in Vegas. Then, in a brilliant instant, my memory hit the jackpot.

"Oh David! David Schiff!" I jumped up from the couch. Suddenly I was awake and squinting at the morning sunshine.

David and his wife, Jenny, had rented space from my last employer. They worked for a different company, but their office had been next to mine. They were two of the kindest people I'd ever met—always thoughtful and caring, always looking for a way to help someone. They were fascinating people too—well-read, lifelong learners, teaching classes in all kinds of things from aviation to self-defense.

I had missed their sweet smiles. What a blessing to hear David's voice. It had been almost a year since we'd talked.

After a brief synopsis of the latest personal news, David told me he and Jenny were starting a new business. They needed a marketing brochure and help with some promotions. He asked if I would be willing to give them a proposal.

We made an appointment for the following day.

I was thankful for the call, but rent was due the day after tomorrow. Even if I got the contract, I wouldn't see a check for at least thirty days. By then I'd be locked into another miserable job, and all my hopes of writing would only be a memory. But I needed every dollar bill, no matter when it came my way. So I pulled out my calculator, sat down at the computer, and wrote out a proposal for my friends.

The next day I drove to David and Jenny's with tissue in my hand and a lump in my throat. I was looking forward to seeing them again, but dreading the start of my last writing project—another chapter of my life without a happy ending. God hadn't provided, so now it was obvious. Writing wasn't His will for me.

The tires of my old Toyota rolled to a stop. I opened the door and stepped onto their driveway.

What else would I do for a living? I couldn't think of a thing. Nothing would put a bounce in my step the way writing had this past year. But now that bounce had vanished like a tulip in a snow-storm.

A big wooden door loomed in front of me. I raised my arm and knocked.

The door opened and Bart was bounding, wagging his fluffy golden retriever tail. Jenny clung to his collar as she looked up and smiled. "Come on in, Patti!"

A rush of joy swept over me. For a fleeting moment I was back in the office chatting with David and Jenny about venturing out on my own. In those days I faced self-employment with all the innocence and eagerness of Bart. Although it seemed like a lifetime since I'd seen her, Jenny hadn't changed a bit. She reached over to give me a hug. David was in the kitchen, pouring one more cup of coffee. He knew I took cream and only half a packet of sweetener.

"It's so good to see you again!" I said.

"I can't believe it's been so long!" Jenny replied, "We've got a lot to catch up on!"

We sat down at the kitchen table, coffee cups in hand, and reminisced about our years as daytime neighbors. I didn't say a word about my financial struggles. I was too embarrassed to admit that I had failed. Plus, I didn't want them to think that because no one would hire me, I wasn't any good.

Soon David began to tell me about their business and the plans they'd made to get it off the ground. Then he asked to see my pro-posal.

I reached into my briefcase and gave them each a copy. Jenny opened the cover and asked me to explain.

Line-by-line, I waded through as I shared my thoughts and described my calculations. When I had finished, David nodded at Jenny. "Looks good to me. What do you think?"

Jenny smiled and agreed.

My heart skipped a beat as David pulled out a pen, opened a checkbook, and wrote my name.

"We always pay a third up front," he said as he tore the check from its stub and handed it to me. It was more than enough to cover rent, utilities, and a refrigerator full of groceries.

I scrambled for every bit of self-control I possessed, nonchalantly reached for the check, folded it in half, and slipped it into my purse. Then I asked about deadlines.

I made it to the car before I burst into tears. When my tears were dry, I sat for a moment in awe. How had this happened? What had God done? How could I have been so wrong?

But I smiled. I had been right about one thing. God had set me up all right, but not to watch me drown. He had set me up to reveal Himself to me in a brand new way!

And now I could see it so clearly. He put me in a place where I had no money, no work, and no hope of paying my rent. He backed me into a corner and took away my options—everything I would normally run to, everything but Him. When He was finally center stage and had my full attention, He let me watch Him work in a way I'd have never predicted. He showed me that He was faithful, powerful, and compassionate. He showed that He would do miracles to prove His love for me.

God had not forgotten me. His eye was on every detail. He knew what was in my kitchen cupboards and how much rent was due. He knew His purpose for my life, and He knew what I needed to get the job done. In fact, He knew I needed assurance that He was the One who had called me to write. What's more, I needed to know that He would make a way for me to do it.

That day I learned, beyond a doubt, that, "Faithful is He who calls you, and He also will bring it to pass" (1 Thessalonians 5:24).

What a lesson! What a blessing to watch my God provide. What a comfort to know that the God of the universe was watching out for me!

I rummaged through my purse to find another tissue, tilted the rearview mirror, and dabbed at the corners of my eyes.

I'd stop by the bank on the way home.

As I checked my mascara, I thought about a project I hadn't yet begun. It was big—too big for me. But God had just shown me that He can do miracles, and whenever He opens the door, He will see me through.

So maybe it was time to start thinking about a title—a title for a book about God.

I had a funny feeling that someday I would need it.

Faithful is He who calls you,
and He also will bring it to pass.
1 THESSALONIANS 5:24

the open door

▶ *"Sixty seconds!"* The producer's voice boomed from the speaker.

I squirmed in my seat. My stomach churned as it wrestled the three gooey fudge brownies I had just devoured. I had been too nervous to eat anything else all day.

What possessed me to agree to this? What in the world was I thinking?

I had been so sure that God was opening a door—another chance for me to speak and write. But now it was clear that this door was a booby trap. Unfortunately, it was way too late to turn around and run.

It had all begun so innocently. Randy asked, I said yes, and here I sat—waiting for the little red dot on my microphone to light up and launch me into my role as a guest on a live radio talk show.

But that wasn't the half of it! It was February 14, and the topic was "Surviving Singleness on Valentine's Day." Now *there* was something I wanted to admit to the world: not only did I have nothing better to do tonight than talk about being single, but I was also about to admit to everyone in a five-state audience that I hadn't had a date on Valentine's Day for the past four years.

I must have lost my marbles.

The second hand raced around its track.

My heart pounded. My head swam. My eyes frantically darted around the room looking for a way to escape.

Too late.

"Three…two…" The producer's voice roared. The second hand swept across the twelve. The music swelled.

I froze in my chair, listened to my heart pound, and tried not to hyperventilate. Four of us were sitting on the panel that evening. Randy and John were friends from Sunday school. I had met Nancy two months earlier at a singles Christmas dance.

"…and the fourth member of our panel is Patti Gordon." The host's voice caught me by surprise.

"It's…good to be here," I choked out, followed by a silent prayer of confession. I hadn't told a whopper like that in ages.

Randy smiled at me from across the table.

What? Was he living on another planet? He looked like he didn't have a care in the world. In fact, he actually looked like he was having fun! Sixty seconds earlier he'd been laughing and joking with John, seemingly oblivious to the fact that at any minute we could all become the laughingstock of the entire southeastern United States.

"…and our first caller is James from Montgomery, Alabama."

I was going to throw up.

The producer was in the control room behind a plate glass window. Maybe if I got his attention, he would let me slip out of the studio and hightail it to the restroom at the end of the hall.

But wait. A reflection caught my eye. It was not the reflection of a grown woman fidgeting with her hair and gnawing at her perfectly manicured nails. A little girl was staring back at me. Her bangs were too short, and her earlobes peeked from beneath that dreadful haircut her mom insisted was so cute.

I knew that little girl. Even though she was fully aware that her hair made her look like the Little Dutch Boy, her brown eyes were smiling. She knew her day would come, for she had big dreams for her life and was willing to work hard to make them come true.

I was eleven years old and thought I could do anything. Back then I had dreamed of being a public speaker for as long as I could remember. I'd seen lots of speakers on TV. When they talked, they stirred things up inside of people. They got people to feed the hungry and build houses for the poor. Some of them even ended wars. They made me want to be a better Christian, a better American, a better citizen of the world.

Whenever I heard a public speaker, I wanted to stand up and say something too. I wanted to inspire somebody, encourage somebody, make somebody laugh. I wanted to help them do better, be better, and then go out and do something wonderful for somebody else. Oh, I thought about being a doctor or a nurse or even an engineer, but my sixth-grade intuition just knew that public speaking was the right career for me.

Miss Bennett, my teacher, had chosen five kids from the speech competition to deliver a three-minute talk during our sixth-grade open house. Both sixth-grade classes and their parents would be there. I wasn't all that surprised to find my name on the list of those who had been chosen. I was one of the "smart kids" in class. It's not that I was all that bright; I just worked really hard. I wanted my mom and dad to be proud of me. But even more, I wanted to get good enough grades so I could go to college, meet a nice boy, and get married someday. Oh yes, I was a highly motivated scholar.

For weeks before the open house, I spent every spare moment in front of the bathroom mirror practicing my speech. It was on nuclear war—pretty heady stuff for a sixth-grader. But with the help of the Encyclopedia Britannica, one newspaper article, and a few words of wisdom from Dad, I ended up with a pretty comprehensive exposé on "Nuclear War in the Twentieth Century."

I studied myself in the mirror as I spoke. The expressions and hand motions were perfectly choreographed. I was especially proud of the part where I made a fist with my right hand and kind of punched the air in front of me with a small sweeping motion to the left. At the same time, I furrowed my brow. The effect was magnificent. It conveyed a mature presentation—as if my convictions were based upon years of careful thought and research.

One Friday night I had been changing channels and saw a woman in a long black dress singing. At the end of her song, she took an elegant bow. It occurred to me that a bow would be just the right way to end my speech. So, arms outstretched, bending from the hips until my back was parallel with the floor, I practiced and practiced until I could do it exactly like she did. Even though I was giving a speech instead of singing a song, I thought it would add a more professional touch.

I spent hours and hours rehearsing. Of course, the bathroom door had to be locked to avoid interruptions. Because I shared that room with five sisters, I wasn't the most popular kid in the house during this time. But it would be worth it.

The day of open house finally arrived. Up at the crack of dawn, I locked myself in the bathroom and began rehearsing. Time flew, and before I knew it the sounds of Saturday morning cartoons drifted from the family room. I knew the routine. A fight was imminent. My sisters would soon be pounding on the door and crying for Mom to make me let them in.

Maybe it was an innate sense of fairness and compassion that touched me that morning. Maybe it was the responsibility I felt as an older, more mature sister to set an example as to how we should love one another. Or maybe it was just the clanging of pots and pans and the smell of sizzling bacon wafting up the stairs that convinced me to surrender my fortress this final morning—without a fight—and mosey on down to the kitchen.

After breakfast, I brushed my teeth and carefully donned my red and white striped shirt and blue corduroy jumper. I disappeared into the closet, rummaged through the dirty socks and T-shirts that had missed the laundry basket, and emerged with the dreaded black tied shoes. They were one of the heaviest crosses I had to bear in sixth grade.

Because there were six girls in our family and money was tight, each of us only got one pair of shoes a year. They were always sensible shoes—buckled or tied so they wouldn't slip off and black or brown so they would go with everything. Each year we pleaded with Mom for the pink pair in the window or the purple slip-ons in the display case, but no amount of conniving or temper tantrum-throwing ever got us the shoes we really wanted. Each year we all walked out of the store with buckled or tied, black or brown shoes with plenty of room in the toe.

This year I found myself at yet another "awkward stage." My feet had grown to women's sizes, but the rest of me had not. Unfortunately, this year I had also discovered that the women's shoe department did not carry a wide selection of sixth-grade-variety,

buckled or tied, black or brown shoes. In fact, the sales clerk could
only find three pairs of "sensible shoes" that passed Mom's inspection.

Two pairs were rather plain buckled shoes—not exactly
fashion-magazine material, but acceptable for a sixth-grade classroom nonetheless. The third was the ugliest pair of black tied shoes
I had ever seen. They were big and clunky with rounded toes,
when all the girls at school were wearing cute little pointy-toed
shoes. They looked like they would survive several hundred thousand walks to school and at least a million toe drags in the circle
around the merry-go-round. Industrial strength shoes. The only
thing that horrified me more than the thought of them lasting for
centuries was the fact that my grandmother had a pair that looked
just like them.

I tried on each pair of kind-of-cuter buckled shoes and duti-
fully walked around the room. Then the clerk pulled the black
monsters out of a box and heartlessly tied them on my feet. After
I stood up and toured around the room again, Mom asked me the
dreaded question. "Which shoes are the most comfortable, Patti?"

I swallowed hard. Telling the truth that day was one of the
bravest things I had ever done. I knew what would happen. Sure
enough, I walked out of the women's shoe department as the not-
so-proud owner of the most comfortable pair of black tied shoes I
had ever worn.

The fallout from my moment of truthfulness began the first
day of school. Our bus was a little late, so the rest of the class was
already seated when we arrived. Teachers always put Don
VanDoren in the front row since the day in fourth grade when he
had crawled out the window when the teacher wasn't looking and
no one could find him the rest of the afternoon. I hadn't seen Don

since last May. It was evident he had grown a lot over the summer, and from the look on his face, I was afraid he had gotten a lot meaner too.

Don took one look at my shoes and smiled that horrible smile that meant somebody would probably be crying by the end of the day. He gave a long, low wolf whistle as I stepped inside the door. Miss Bennett called his first and last name very sternly and kindly pointed me toward my new desk. I could hear Don's snickers. My face began to burn as I sheepishly made my way down a row of giggling classmates. At recess he dubbed my shoes "Patti's black boats." Unfortunately, the name caught on with some of the other boys, and recess was pretty miserable for a couple of weeks until Margo Mendez got a bad haircut and braces on the same day.

Every time I put those shoes on, something inside me cringed, but today I pulled them on and tied them without flinching. Today I would redeem myself. I would stand in front of the whole sixth grade class and their families, and they wouldn't even notice my shoes. They would be listening, with rapt attention, to the brilliance of my oratorical skills. After today, those boys would be sorry they ever made fun of me. After today, it would be clear that I was destined for greatness.

Finally it was time to leave for the open house. Outside the sun was shining, and the smell of spring rose from the damp ground. The daffodils Mom planted last year waved their yellow hats goodbye as six Gordon girls followed Dad down the sidewalk and piled into the station wagon. I huddled in the corner of the backseat, whispering my speech into the window until we pulled up to a red brick building with wide steps and a big front door.

Dad opened the car door, and we poured onto the sidewalk. Mom gathered us around for her "public place" speech. First, she told us all to act like ladies. Then she instructed the three big girls to hold a little sister's hand. We always had to hold hands whenever we went into a grocery store, library, or any other public place. Mom said she could keep track of three pairs of girls a lot better than six individual kids running around. But I think she paired us up because it was a lot harder to get into trouble with only one free hand and a tattletale sister at your side.

I marched to the front of the Gordon clan—little sister in tow—and proudly paraded up the steps and down the shiny-floored hall that smelled like too much bathroom cleaner. At last, we stepped through big double doors with "Gymnasium" posted above.

Inside the gym, sixth-graders and their families milled about. The first two rows were reserved for the speech-givers and their families. I proudly led my family to their chairs, sat down at the end of my row, and mentally began to review my speech—just one more time.

"*Shhhh*s" filled the room.

Miss Bennett stood at the front. Miss Bennett was beautiful— tall and slender—and she always wore the prettiest clothes. I kept track once. She could go three weeks without wearing the same thing twice. But best of all, her shoes always matched. Miss Bennett had blue shoes, red shoes and beige shoes with black trim. She had shoes with the toes cut out, shoes with the heels cut out, and shoes with nothing cut out. I wanted to be just like Miss Bennett when I grew up.

She welcomed the families and told them how proud she was of all her students. I worked hard so Miss Bennett would be proud of me. She was my favorite teacher ever, and I wanted to do my very best for her.

Before I knew it, she was introducing Jimmy Edwards. We were going in alphabetical order, so with an *E* for Edwards, Jimmy was the first speaker. I would be next with a *G* for Gordon. I was glad God had given me a last name at the beginning of the alphabet. I couldn't wait to get up there and show everyone how well I could do.

Jimmy walked stiffly to the front of the room and turned to face the crowd. His voice shook a little as he spoke on acid rain. He had done a lot of research, but his voice was starting to change, and every so often he squeaked. You could tell it embarrassed him because his face would turn red and he would look down—but each time he kept on going.

I had heard Jimmy's speech before, so after a little while I just pretended to listen. My attention turned to the more important task of finding out where all my friends were sitting. Susie Stanley and her family were just a few feet away. Susie had had a slumber party at her house last Friday night. We stayed up all night dancing and telling each other which boys we wanted to kiss.

Jimmy droned on. I shifted in my seat.

Polly Olsen and her mom were not far from Susie. They lived in our neighborhood, so Polly and I walked home from school together. We stopped at Polly's house first since her mom always had warm brownies or chocolate chip cookies waiting for us to eat as soon as we walked in the door. Polly had become a *very* good friend of mine.

As my eyes scanned dozens of unfamiliar faces, the palms of my hands began to get moist. I wiped them across my jumper.

Louis Simmons was two rows back. He had flunked third grade, so he was a year older and the tallest boy in class. I had a crush on him, but he never paid attention to me. He was always teasing Cindy Johnston. She had long blond hair and wore really short skirts to school. I was at a definite disadvantage with a mom who could sew and cut hair.

Jimmy finished speaking, and the crowd erupted into a round of applause. The guys he ate lunch with were whistling loudly and cheering in the back row.

No one had ever cheered like that for me. This was going to be a tough act to follow.

Jimmy made his way back to his seat, and Miss Bennett returned to the front of the room. She announced my name. Everybody clapped.

Suddenly I didn't want to stand up.

Suddenly I didn't want to do anything except sit in my seat and let Rusty Jackson go next. What was happening? I'd looked forward to this for weeks!

But Miss Bennett had already introduced me, so I didn't have a choice. I struggled to my feet, made the corners of my mouth bend into a smile, and shuffled to the front of the room. I gazed for a moment at a pair of big black boats, then turned and looked into a field of faces—every one of them staring straight at me.

My knees began to tremble.

Then I heard it…

Ba-bum. Ba-bum. Ba-bum. My heart.

I never knew I could hear my heart when I was standing still. The only other times I had heard it were when my cousin Greg tried to squirt me with a garden hose or when Sammy Russell chased me across the playground with a dead worm. But this was my heart all right, and it was beating so loudly that I could hardly think.

Why am I so nervous? I thought. *I know this speech like the back of my hand! I'm sure I'll calm down as soon as I get started.*

I wiped my palms across my jumper and opened my mouth. I

formed the words and heard a trembling voice—a very, very soft voice.

Who in the world is that? It can't be me! I talk so loud that even grandpa can hear.

I could see my mother in the second row leaning forward, straining to listen.

"On August 6, 1945, an atomic bomb was dropped on Hiroshima, Japan. Two days later…"

Pitiful. Just pitiful.

This wasn't how it was supposed to be! This wasn't the strong, self-confident Patti Gordon I'd been watching in the bathroom mirror week after week. This timid little girl could barely be heard over the sound of the air conditioner.

The pounding in my head continued as I haltingly began paragraph two.

"Before President Roosevelt died, he hadn't committed to…"

Get a grip on yourself, Patti. Maybe you should close your eyes…

That didn't help. I could still see those faces in my mind, and I probably looked like I was praying.

I will be calm soon. I will get a hold of myself, launch into a riveting performance, and everyone will forget about my weak start. Then they'll be impressed. It's not too late. Maybe I should try the hand motions.

I knew those hand motions backward and forward, but suddenly I had no control over my body. At first my arms were stiff. Then they felt like rubber. All the while they were shaking like two palm branches in a hurricane.

Okay. Hand motions are out. Maybe if I concentrate on my voice, I can still pull this one off.

But no matter how hard I tried, my voice continued to shake. The louder it got, the stronger the vibrato. I sounded like an opera singer on a public television show. But at least the words continued to roll off my tongue…louder…then softer…then louder again. Even though my delivery was horrible, even though I knew Miss Bennett would never pick me for anything else again, even though I'd ruined my only chance to redeem myself after my "big black boats" fiasco, at least my speech was interesting. At least I was making sense.

I was getting close to the bottom of the first page. I knew where all the pages ended. I had studied those four typewritten pages so many hours that I could see them in my mind. The first page had a last minute transition penned across the bottom and up the right margin.

I was moving right along. My mind turned to page two.

Tim Davis and Mike Brown started to giggle. They were sitting in the first row, right in front of me. Tim's mom reached over and grabbed his arm. Behind him, Bobby Kingston brought a blue plastic straw to his mouth. I knew a spit wad was getting ready to fly. This couldn't get any worse.

But wait…

What was happening? I could see page two in my mind…but I couldn't remember the words. What came next? I had two more pages to go. This was supposed to be a three-minute speech, and I had barely finished the first sixty seconds.

I carefully recited the last sentence of page one. Page two would come. I knew it would—just like it had hundreds of times in front of the bathroom mirror.

Hang on, Patti. You can do it. Don't choke. You know this.

The last word of page one echoed through the gymnasium.

My mouth stopped. I stood in disbelief.

My mind was totally blank.

I had no idea what the next word was supposed to be, no idea how the next section was supposed to start, no clue what the rest of my speech was about.

I froze.

Seconds crawled as I stood in front of that gymnasium full of people. My face burned. My heart pounded. My eyes darted through the sea of faces searching for someone—anyone—who could help me. There was Susie Stanley's dad. He leaned forward slowly in his chair, eyebrows raised, lips parted. It was as if he would say the words for me if he could. But even Susie Stanley's dad didn't know the next word of my speech. He had been so nice last Saturday morning when he drove us all to get doughnuts after the slumber party. Now I was humiliated. I could never go to Susie's house again.

Polly's mom was in the front row. When my eyes met hers, she looked down at her hands in her lap. She wouldn't even look at me. *She must think I'm stupid.* How could I ever face her again?

I hung my head, stared at the ugliest pair of black tied shoes I had ever seen, and listened to an eternity of silence.

Then Don VanDoren started to snicker somewhere in the back of the room. I would know that snicker anywhere. Two or three of his friends joined in, and suddenly I realized that recess wasn't going to be any fun for a very, very long time.

I looked to my right and saw the door to the playground—I could see freedom through the glass above the push bar. My mind raced. It was an easy exit. All I wanted to do was run out those doors. A short fifteen to twenty feet, and I wouldn't have to look at those faces in the audience. But in my heart I knew I couldn't leave. That would make things even worse. I would be branded a coward, and a *stupid* coward at that. My face got hotter and hotter.

It took every ounce of strength to keep my shoes firmly planted and listen to the shuffle of feet and muffled coughs. There was no running away from these people. There was no running away from the fact that I had failed. I was no longer "Patti Gordon, the smart girl with the ugly black tied shoes." From this point forward I would be "Patti Gordon, the girl with the ugly black tied shoes who couldn't even remember a three-minute speech."

A word…wait…a sentence. It was coming to me now. It was the last paragraph of my speech, but nobody else knew that. I was hanging on to anything that could get me off that stage—anything that could get me away from my misery and, from the looks on the faces in front of me, the misery of my audience.

I heard a voice—soft at first—hesitating, then gaining momentum as I spoke faster and faster—careening toward the last word of the final paragraph. When I got to it I would be free. Free to sit down. Free to hope that no one would talk to me after the program was over. Free to pray that Mom and Dad wouldn't try to comfort me like they always did. I never wanted to hear about this again. I would be free all right. Free until Monday at recess.

I finished the speech, crept back to my seat, and cried and cried when I got home.

Nineteen years later, I could still feel the shame of that moment. And here I was, minutes from doing it all over again. The only thing I didn't know was how long it would take my mind to go completely blank this time.

James from Alabama was on the phone telling his story. Randy, John, and Nancy listened intently.

His story had a familiar ring. I'd been through something similar, and God had used it to teach me a powerful lesson.

I needed to tell James about it. I needed to speak up.

But how?

I could almost feel the cold stiffness of those black tied shoes on my feet. I could almost hear the taunts of the boys at recess as they pointed their fingers, covered their mouths, and giggled as I walked by. I could still feel the shame of my failure and the disappointment of watching my dream turn to ashes.

But James…

As the voice on the telephone tugged at my heart, an inkling of revelation sifted through my mind.

It wasn't about whether I would succeed or fail. It wasn't about proving my talent or intelligence. In fact, it wasn't even about whether people would admire or make fun of me. As I listened to that sweet Alabama drawl, I realized that God's call to write and speak wasn't about me at all.

It never was. It never would be.

It was about James and others like him with the same questions and the same heartache. It was about God wanting to give them encouragement and give me the blessing of being used by Him. All God asked was that I walk in obedience—even in spite of my fears.

Then a verse came to mind:

"Do not worry about how or what you are to say; for it will be given you in that hour what you are to say. For it is not you who speak, but it is the Spirit of your Father who speaks in you." (Matthew 10:19–20)

Then another:

I can do all things through Him who strengthens me. (Philippians 4:13)

I breathed a long, slow sigh and felt the comfort of that simple truth wrap itself around me. He always told me just what I needed, just when I needed it most.

Yes, God knew my fears. He knew my limitations. He knew that at this moment my tongue felt like the Mojave Desert and my armpits resembled Niagara Falls. He knew that my mind froze whenever I got nervous. He knew how I scraped and scrambled, yet could never find the right words to say. He knew that the only time I thought of something clever was *after* everyone had gone home. Yes, He knew every weakness. He knew every detail. He knew how horribly equipped I was to open my mouth and speak in public.... He knew because He made me that way.

He also knew I needed a reminder that I didn't have to do it on my own. He would be there. He would help me, and through my weakness He'd glorify Himself. Yes, He would give me everything I needed to accomplish what He asked me to do.

My eyes closed as I prayed for courage; then a sense of calmness washed over me. I opened my eyes to a peace and assurance that God would do what I could not. I smiled at Randy and nodded to the host to let him know I'd take this one.

James from Alabama finished his story. I leaned toward the microphone, took a deep breath,...

And spoke.

I can do all things through Him who strengthens me.
PHILIPPIANS 4:13

bigger fish to fry

▶ *Screeeeeeeeech!*

Brake to the floorboard, heart in my throat, I careened forward.

Closer…closer…closer…

Stop.

I sighed, shrank back into the seat, and thanked God.

I was inches—just inches away from a sickening thud, a red-faced, fist-shaking casualty, and a whopping insurance bill.

It would have been completely my fault. I looked down at my trembling hand still clutching the classifieds and thought about the poor guy in the Mercedes in front of me. He must've been cussing up a blue streak by now. And who could blame him? He had almost been flattened by an over-caffeinated bargain hunter in a home decorating frenzy.

I sheepishly tried to avert the glares from my preempted whiplash victim.

Finally I looked up. "Sorry!" I mouthed, scrunching my shoulders and lifting my palms. I really was.

More glares.

When would that light turn green?

There. Cars were moving. The guy in the Mercedes was going straight. Maybe I'd just take a right.

One quick turn and I was winding through a neighborhood of gentle hills crowned with castle-like dwellings. Morning sunlight stretched long shadows down meandering driveways and perfectly manicured lawns. Talk about home sweet home! These were some of Atlanta's finest.

I'd *love* the key to one of those front doors hanging from my silver key chain. I'd love to wake up, walk into the backyard, and slip into my own heated pool. I'd love to serve dinner on a ten-foot-long table beneath a crystal chandelier. Truth was, I'd love all kinds of expensive things, but for now I'd have to settle for a few bargain baubles from a neighborhood garage sale or two.

Yes, garage saling was a brand-new adventure for me, but I was getting the hang of it fast. Mom told me rule number one: go to garage sales in the wealthy part of town. I had just figured out rule number two: don't read garage sale ads while you're driving. Other than that, it was pretty straightforward: "One man's trash is another man's treasure." Now, that was my kind of recycling plan!

You see, I loved nice things and I loved to decorate, but I didn't have a lot of extra money. I was saving my cash for a couple of dreams, so garage sale hopping to spruce up my apartment was about as far as I would let myself go. I'd learned in seventh grade that to get what you want, sometimes you have to give up a few things. Back then I wanted more than a dozen shades of nail polish and weekly matinee movie tickets. I had other ambitions—grander goals, bigger fish to fry.

So I saved my allowance and babysitting money and bought my first wool suit. I loved to hear the whisper of its taffeta lining and open my closet door just to see the jacket sleeve peeking from between the blouses. I held my head high every time I slipped it on and fastened its shiny gold buttons.

Since then my taste had moved up a notch. Now I wanted more than a fashionable wardrobe, a new set of dishes, and a bathroom full of fluffy towels. I had other ambitions—grander goals, bigger fish to fry.

This time I wanted a mortgage.

I wanted to paint a wall without asking permission. I wanted to clean my own garage. I wanted to complain about mowing the lawn, paying property taxes, and replacing the furnace. I wanted to drag a big green trash can out to the curb every Friday morning. I wanted the American Dream, by golly, and I was determined to get it! At the rate I was saving, I'd have my down payment in three more penny-pinching years.

But even though I was well on my way to buying a home of my own, I had other ambitions, grander goals—I wanted a wedding dress someday. If I could find a man before I bought a house, I could use my down-payment money to pay for a big, fancy wedding. I'd been dating Joe Martin for almost three months. He was handsome, had a great job, and was paying an awful lot of attention to me. Joe was charming and a wonderful dresser. He drove a sports car and had a beautiful home. He always had tickets to the theater or symphony. Sometimes he went to church; sometimes he didn't (but we could work on that). Right now I was having a marvelous time, and things were looking pretty promising.

But there was just one problem—one snag in sight. After three months of dating, the moment of truth had finally arrived. I'd hemmed and hawed, beat around the bush, and finally run out of excuses. There was no more stalling. No getting around it. Joe was coming over for a home-cooked meal tonight.

I dreaded this part of the dating cycle. It was when men finally found out that cooking was not my forte. I'd studied all about it in Home Ec classes but never enjoyed it enough to actually do it. I survived on baked chicken, microwaved entrees, and plates of steamed vegetables topped with mounds of cottage cheese.

Oh, I always tried to focus on the brighter side—no one would gain weight at *my* dinner table. But every man wants a home-cooked meal eventually. So now was the time to try it again. One desperate phone call to my older sister, Margie, and I had a recipe that she promised was foolproof.

But that was yet to be seen.

Tonight was the night. Joe would be knocking on my door at seven, and I'd be praying that we wouldn't have to listen to the smoke alarm all evening.

So in the likely case that dinner didn't quite live up to Joe's expectations, I had figured out another way to let him know what a wonderful wife I'd be. If I couldn't impress him with my culinary genius, I'd wow him with my flair for interior design. A garage-sale spree would help gussy things up without robbing too much from the wedding fund. If Joe saw I had other domestic talents, maybe he would overlook a black and crunchy pea or two.

Patti Martin. It had a nice ring to it. *I wonder if he wants children.*

Up ahead a bright yellow sign beckoned me with big black letters: *Estate Sale.*

Wow! I'd never been to one of those before. Everyone said they were a bargain hunter's dream! Finding a sign in this neighborhood felt like I'd stumbled across the end of a rainbow. Now, off to find that big pot of gold!

The address was at the bottom of the sign, so I pumped the brake and pulled to the curb. A minute with my map showed that the "estate" was less than two blocks away.

This couldn't get any easier.

I searched for numbers on elegant mailboxes that drifted by as I drove. Finally, the car rolled to a stop, and I peered up a hill. The house was magnificent. This couldn't be it. I double-checked the back of the Krispy Kreme napkin: 4227... Sure enough! A grin spread from ear to ear as I surveyed my new hunting grounds.

My ten-year-old Toyota slipped into a space behind a long line of parked cars. It was only a few minutes past eight, but it looked like at least a dozen people had beaten me to the punch. I'd better get in there before the good stuff was gone.

I scurried along the driveway and up to the front door.

It was ajar. I knocked. No response.

My fingers gave a wary push. I peered inside.

No one in sight.

I peeked around the corner, timidly stepped onto a lustrous marble floor, and gazed into a towering foyer. An elegant staircase clung to the wall, flaunting a graceful mahogany banister. My eyes climbed through a sparkling chandelier hanging from a ceiling medallion.

It was amazing.

Oh, I could just see myself opening the door to the astonished faces of all my friends! I'd listen to their *ooooh*s and *ahhh*s and humbly respond, "Oh, thank you," and, "Yes, we enjoy it." I imagined floating down that staircase in a beaded evening gown as Joe and his admiring eyes waited at the bottom.

It was official. This was the life for me.

Gaping archways beckoned me into a spacious living room. Murky green rectangles dotted the walls—just a shade darker than the rest of the paint. I wondered whose portrait had hung above the fireplace. Oh, if mine could only hang in a home like this one day!

Faded velvet draperies dripping with gold fringe framed the yawning windows. They must have been incredibly elegant in their time. Broad wooden molding crowned a lofty ceiling. Satin hardwood floors lay at my feet.

Long folding tables stretched across the room laden with the pickings of plundered cupboards, shelves, and drawers. Some things were just junk. Others were mysterious treasures—a cut-glass vase, old picture frames, an antique jewelry box—all pregnant with stories of their own.

A handful of strangers shuffled silently along, picking up items, turning them over, and then carefully placing them back in their spots. Now and then a stranger smiled, tucked a treasure in the crook of an arm, and continued down the row.

I ventured to the field of tables to begin my harvest. Crystal candlesticks, a silver butter dish, a Blue Willow serving bowl. Surely these things would impress Joe tonight! What was that? A cobalt blue pitcher?

Piece by piece, my collection grew.

I smiled and surveyed the treasures stretched before me, when a twinkle of enchantment caught my eye. I reverently approached a glimmering monument, a peek at past life in the palace.

My, my! This one was a beauty.

The graceful vessels of a silver tea service tiptoed on a sterling tray. I gently lifted the teapot and toasted the days it shared its sweet nectar with women dressed in tasteful finery and fashionable feathered hats.

How many hours had it patiently guarded raspberry scones and lemon curd while listening to the stories of little blue-haired ladies? How many times had it bowed to bring a hot cup of comfort on a cold winter night?

I glanced at the price tag, shook my head, and vowed that someday Joe and I would own one just like it.

A few feet away, a pair of antique reading glasses stared up from the table. What stories had entered those glistening gates? What worlds of wonder had they introduced to the one on whose nose they perched for hours? Whom did they enlighten? Whom did they amuse? Whose monogrammed handkerchief wiped them clean?

Who knew?

Someday, I too would spend hours on a fancy sofa, perched in front of a roaring fire, sipping from delicate, hand-painted cups, uncovering the secrets of a fascinating book. Oh, I'd live in the lap of luxury. It was only a matter of time.

I meandered to a mountain of leather-bound books. *Georgia Code—Annotated—1943.* The cover creaked open. *Alfred Lawrence Brooks* was prominently stamped on the first yellowed page.

So Mr. Brooks was a lawyer—and a good one at that judging from the grandeur of his home. How many hours had he pored through these books looking for a case or a phrase to make his point? How many clients had peered across his desk and worried about how big their bill would be? How many people would've paid any price for the help and protection of Alfred Lawrence Brooks?

I tucked the leather volume under my arm—a reminder that I too must work hard.

I wandered to the kitchen. More tables, more treasures. Monogrammed napkins, fine china, glistening goblets. Did friends love to dine at Mr. Brooks' table? Someday I'd host dinner parties for friends and family too! We'd eat the finest food off the most expensive china. There'd be silver salt and pepper shakers for every single guest. I would love hearing brilliant stories and rounds of pealing laughter ringing from my crystal chandelier.

A white linen table cloth, a gleaming candelabra... Did Mr. Brooks adore his wife? Would Joe adore me too? Would we sit, for hours, and talk about the future? Would candlelight dinners keep our romance alive?

Turning, I faced a staircase in the corner of the kitchen. I climbed each step, wandered the hallways, and peered through open doors. I passed a collection of tiny treasures—lives laid bare in trinkets on tables. Bracelets, necklaces, a monogrammed locket—were they secrets of golden boxes underneath a Christmas tree or cherished souvenirs of a romantic evening?

Oh, someday I'd have boxes of jewelry and closets full of fancy clothes.

Four majestic posts and a magnificent headboard guarded an oversized mattress. Did Mr. Brooks sleep soundly knowing that all was well? Did he toss and turn at night with worries of tomorrow? Was he resting soundly now? Were his worries over? Was he lying in a nursing home or lying in a coffin?

I froze. My shoulders wilted.

What in the world was I thinking? Why did I ask that question? Why would that morbid thought even cross my mind?

I tried to ignore it, to pretend it didn't matter. Yet it lingered like a storm cloud in the air.

I peered into another room and another and another.

I leaned over and inspected the filigreed lace on a white linen bed skirt and matching pillow case. I studied the intricate carving on the drawers of an antique mahogany dresser. I examined the satin piping on a set of embroidered finger towels.

But everything I saw begged the same hard question: "Where was Mr. Brooks now?"

I finally surrendered to the unrelenting question, retreated from the bedroom, and crept back down the stairs.

Yes. Where was he now?

And where would I be if I continued to focus on the things my eyes could see.

I sensed a silent whisper:

You are just a vapor that appears for a little while and then vanishes away. (James 4:14)

At the bottom of the stairs I stopped to ponder the truth of that simple verse. If my life continued in the direction it was heading, what would I have left when all was said and done?

I wandered through an elegant game room and surveyed a lifetime of treasures. Had he vanished? Was he gone? Was he at peace or in turmoil? Was his heart still beating, or had it come to rest?

If his heart was at rest, when would I join him? When was I destined to stand before the Lord?

If Mr. Brooks had met the Lord, had he been afraid? Did he meet a friend, or did he meet a stranger? When he lived his life on earth, did he invest it wisely? Did he use his wealth and power for treasures that would last?

I hoped so.

For his earthly treasures were useless to him now as they disappeared in a gust of greedy strangers. His memory would live on with friends and family for a season, but even they would vanish like a vapor one day.

Then what would be left of Alfred Lawrence Brooks?

I paused in the living room, paid for my collection, then slipped through the towering foyer and out the open door. Halfway down the hill I turned around and gazed at a brick and mortar monument to a mentor I had never met.

The car door opened, and I slid into the front seat and laid my collection of treasures next to me. I fingered the tattered edges of a leather-bound book, a reminder of a lesson Mr. Brooks had taught me well.

The rich man in the midst of his pursuits will fade away. (James 1:11)

When God created the things of this world He said that they were "good." He gave them to us as gifts to enjoy. But there was no denying it. There was no escaping the fact that one day my life on this earth would be over, and I, too, would be forced to leave its treasures behind. Everything my eyes could see, everything my hands could touch, even my body would turn to dust one day.

My fingers glided across the dome of a silver butter dish.

Had I fallen in love with this world? If my next breath would be my last, what would be waiting for me on the other side? How would I feel when my chance to prepare for eternity was over? I couldn't imagine the regret I would feel if that chance had been wasted and all I held was dust.

A handsome couple, with arms full of boxes, strolled down the grassy hill. My eyes traveled a winding walkway that beckoned me back to a massive front door.

But could I abandon my hopes and dreams?

I looked down at a well-worn volume; then opened its cover to the first yellowed page.

Eyes closed, I grieved for a moment. *Yes, I suppose I could…*

Then I gazed again at the mansion on a hill. But this time it looked different. Something about it wasn't quite the same. It had only been a moment since I'd admired it last. The house could not have changed that quickly. Perhaps the change had happened to me.

As I sat in my car and stared at that manor, its enchantment continued to wane. The allure of its riches was fading away. Something deep inside of me was obviously shifting. I was looking at the world from a different point of view.

Now I wasn't quite so sure if I wanted a silver tea service, a glistening chandelier, and a closet full of fancy clothes. It didn't really matter if I wore expensive jewelry, drank from the finest crystal, or ate with a sterling spoon.

The longer I thought, the clearer I saw the world from a different perspective. It didn't make sense to invest my life in things that would last for just a few years. Those years were simply a drop of water in the ocean of eternity. Now I could see that the only thing worth living for was something that would never rust, break, or fade away—something that another hundred years would never find lying in a pile of rubble and regret.

I thought about a lesson I learned in Sunday School. God created the moon and the stars and the mountains and the oceans and the fields to give Him glory. God created me to give Him glory too. That was the ultimate purpose for my life.

As I sat alone in my ten-year-old Toyota, a veil finally lifted and I stared at the truth. I wanted my life to count for something more than a world that would turn to dust one day. Now all I wanted was to live to give God glory, because that was the only thing that would matter in the end.

Then I remembered another lesson. It was one I had learned in seventh grade: Sometimes, to get what you really want, you have to be willing to give up a few things. I thought about Joe—his handsome face, his romantic surprises. I was falling in love with that man, but Joe loved the world and everything in it much more than he loved God. I couldn't imagine him wanting to pray or encouraging me to trust Jesus. I couldn't imagine him studying the Bible or going to church if I wasn't with him. No, Joe was not a man who would help me serve God better. Joe was a man who would keep me focused on things that would fade away.

So I closed my eyes, bowed my head, and surrendered my plans for a home and a husband. Then I asked God to use me for whatever would glorify Him most.

When I lifted my head, I knew that I would never regret that prayer. Maybe God would give me a beautiful home and maybe even a husband. Then again, maybe He wouldn't. But God sees a bigger picture than my finite eyes can see, and He loves me more than I can comprehend. That's quite a combination—one that I can trust.

Years have passed, and time continues to test the promises to God that I have made. And I continue to pray that He will give me the strength and wisdom to be faithful. I beg Him to remind me that these years on earth are fleeting. I implore Him to help me look beyond the things my eyes can see. Oh, I love my life on earth. Don't get me wrong. But I have other ambitions—grander goals, bigger fish to fry.

You are just a vapor that appears for a little while and then vanishes away.
JAMES 4:14

finding

beauty

in the ashes

Sometimes a noble failure serves the world
as faithfully as a distinguished success.

EDWARD DOWDEN

No one knows how to help you in your
times of failure as Jesus does!
He will not overlook your shortcoming or
simply encourage you to do better the next time.
He will give you victory in the midst of your failure.

HENRY T. BLACKABY AND RICHARD BLACKABY
EXPERIENCING GOD DAY-BY-DAY

Let the past sleep, but let it sleep in the sweet embrace of Christ,
and let us go on into the invincible future with Him.

OSWALD CHAMBERS
MY UTMOST FOR HIS HIGHEST DAILY DEVOTIONAL

8

the fight: round 1

▶ *WHAT? No way…*

My eyes strained to focus in the dimly lit elevator. *It must be the light…*

But a closer look assured me it was not.

I stared at the horror-stricken face reflecting from the elevator's shiny doors. *Why this? Why now? This can't be happening.*

But it was.

I closed my eyes and waited for the inevitable. This was supposed to be my first day on the job. Finally! A contract with a Fortune 500 company. This day was going to put my career on the map.

I opened my eyes. The mahogany paneling reeked with opulence, little comfort for what lay ahead.

If only I had known. If only I could go back. Unfortunately, *rewind* was not an option.

Twenty-six…twenty-seven…

The elevator stopped. The doors slid open, and...I stepped into the lobby of my first Fortune 500 client with a blue shoe on one foot and a brown shoe on the other.

Why?

Why, oh, why did I buy the same style in two colors? Why didn't I have the foresight to see the humiliation born of a burned-out bulb in the closet?

I studied my elegant surroundings and tried my best to look confident. But holding my head high as I stood in a cornucopia of shoes was like trying to smile when, all the while, I knew I had a pea in my tooth.

It just wasn't going to happen.

I slunk across the shiny marble floor to a meticulously coiffed and manicured receptionist. I leaned forward and muttered, "Would you please let Jenni Warner know that Patti Gordon is here?"

She looked at me out of the corner of her eye then turned and faced me squarely. "Certainly, Ms. Gordon," she said in a voice that assured me she was wearing two of the shiniest matching shoes I'd ever seen. I slithered toward a black leather chair, sat down, and tried to blend into the wall.

Jenni and I had been on a committee at church together almost a year ago. I liked her the minute we met. Jenni was a whole lot of fun. She was also quite the career woman—a manager for a huge company in town. We had tried to get together for lunch a few times but were never quite able to sync up our schedules.

Then about a month ago, she had given me a call to see if I would be interested in some contract work with her company. Who was she kidding? Of course I'd be interested! I would practically volunteer my services to get a big name like that on my resume. Her team needed help with market research and writing. I showed her my portfolio, and she set up an interview with the hiring manager for the following week.

I had never worked for a big company before and had no idea if my skills were on par. After the interview, I went straight home, choked down some Maalox, and got on my knees. No one was more surprised than I when two weeks later they offered me a six-month contract, with a possible extension to a year. To top it off, the pay was a dream!

Of course, I reacted like any normal woman and headed straight for the mall. I'd been waiting four years for my ship to come in, so by now my meager wardrobe was worn and outdated. Besides, this contract might be my boat to paradise. But that morning, as I stared at the shoe department on my feet and thought about my one chance to make a first impression, it looked like my dinghy was destined to drown.

Twelve families of eight could have checked out of Wal-Mart in the time it took Jenni to make it to the lobby. During that time, at least a dozen executives marched by wearing perfectly pressed suits with stiffly starched shirts and carrying expensive leather briefcases.

This was going to be a rough day.

Finally, Jenni's beaming face appeared—an island of warmth in the middle of frozen tundra. She apologized for taking so long. She had gotten stuck on an emergency conference call.

"That's okay, Jenni. I understand. But would you promise me one thing?" I closed my eyes and pointed at my feet.

"Oh, Patti!" she exclaimed and heartlessly giggled.

"I can't believe I did it, Jenni. Please promise that you won't introduce me to anyone today."

She giggled again and acquiesced. Then she led me to a tiny

office and helped me settle in to start work on the project.

The rest of the day I parked my nose in the computer and planted my feet firmly underneath the desk. One by one, coworkers wandered over to say hello to the new kid on the block. I repeatedly found myself explaining the mystery of the multicolored shoes. By the end of the day, I was laughing along with them. So much for my fears about whether I'd like the people!

The next day, in a big break with tradition, I actually wore matching shoes and made it down the hall a few times. After a couple of hellos in the break room and a team meeting in the afternoon, I was beginning to feel at home. By the end of the week, I couldn't imagine what more a girl could want from Corporate America—interesting work, wonderful people, and a paycheck every two weeks was almost more security and happiness than my little heart could handle!

The next Monday I began a routine of getting to the office early. An off-the-charts morning person, I loved to get to work before the rest of the crowd. It gave me a chance to get ahead of the game and stay out of cardiac rehab by beating the morning traffic. I opened the door to my office, shoved my oversized purse in a drawer, then booted up my computer and began to check e-mail.

Hmm. Who is Aaron Taylor? I mentally reviewed the list of people I'd met last week. I didn't remember an Aaron Taylor on the team, but the name sounded awfully familiar. Oh yes! Of course. He was the director of marketing in the office around the corner. Everyone on my team reported to him or reported to someone who reported to him.

I'd seen him a couple of times in the hallway and two or three times in the break room getting coffee. I always got tongue-tied when he was around. He was about my age, awfully cute, and a very sharp dresser. On top of having the most gorgeous blue eyes, he had to be brilliant to be in his position.

But why would he send me an e-mail? I didn't think he even knew my name. I hoped everything was okay. Did he see the rough draft I'd turned in last week? Maybe he didn't like it. Maybe he didn't think I had what it took. *What if he wants to fire me? I have to earn enough to at least pay the credit card bills for all my new clothes!*

I winced as I clicked on his name.

Patti, I wanted to welcome you personally. I hope you're enjoying working with my team. Let me know if there is anything I
can do to help you with the project. Aaron

I exhaled. *Oh, thank goodness!*
Then I clicked reply.

Thank you so much, Aaron! I really appreciate the welcome! Patti

Send.

What an awesome guy. Talk about southern hospitality at its finest. A director taking time to welcome the temporary help? This company must be a dream.

I smiled, answered a few more e-mails, then headed toward the break room to start the coffee. When I opened the door, I could smell coffee brewing. Someone had already beaten me to the punch. I poked my head in the refrigerator. *Now where's that half-and-half?*

"Good morning, Patti. How was your first week?"

I whirled around. Aaron was standing in the doorway. *Is he talking to me? Well, I'm the only other person in the room, and my name is Patti. Awfully good chance.*

My brain turned to jelly. "Oh, it was great. Thank you, Aaron."

Should I tell him how happy I am to have a steady income for the first time in almost four years? Maybe not.

"I love the project, and everyone's so nice." *Is that all you can say, Patti? Think of something clever—or at least something intelligent. He's going to wonder why they hired you.*

"We've got a great team," Aaron said. "I'm glad you're enjoying them. By the way, how was your weekend?"

I smiled. "Oh, it was wonderful. It was beautiful outside." *Lame, Patti, lame! Don't talk about the weather—anything but the weather. Say something else—quick.*

"Oh, Aaron, thank you for the e-mail," I said. "It made me feel really welcome."

Aaron smiled. "Well, I want to make sure you feel at home here. We're glad to have you."

Thank goodness the coffee had finished brewing and he drank it black. There was no way I could think of enough words to fill the time it took to fiddle with cream and sugar. He grabbed his cup then looked down at my feet.

"Hmm, matching shoes. Nice…"

He smiled, winked at me, then turned toward the door.

Did he just say…? How in the world did he hear about my shoes? How humiliating! How… Oh Patti, chill out. Don't be in such a wad.

I broke into a giggle. "Word sure travels fast around here."

He looked over his shoulder, flashed an impish grin, and was gone.

The next morning we were back in the break room together. *He must be a morning person too.*

Aaron's comment about my shoes had broken the ice, so I was feeling pretty comfortable with him. Besides, I had noticed that he wasn't wearing a wedding ring. *Hmm.*

Day after day, week after week, we'd chat as we waited for the coffee to brew. His office was not far from mine, so if his light was on when I got to work, I'd pop my head in.

"Good morning, Aaron!"

"Good morning, Patti!" He would look up and smile as he greeted me.

Through our little break room chats, I learned that he loved to sail. He spent his summer weekends on a lake not far from Atlanta. After college he'd spent a couple months bicycling through Europe. *What an amazing guy!*

As the months flew by, I began to feel like I really belonged at this company. I loved the project and thoroughly enjoyed everyone on the team. Another wonderful part of the experience was the friendship I was developing with Jenni. We grabbed lunch together on a regular basis and told each other all kinds of things about our families, the men we had dated, and our struggles with being single. I couldn't imagine a better place to work and prayed that God would let me stay there for years.

It was another Monday morning, and I'd just gotten back from my break-room chat with Aaron.

Bling.

Oh, an e-mail from Aaron. I hadn't gotten one from him since his welcome my first week. Was there a problem with the project?

Click.

I enjoy our chats in the morning, Patti. I'm glad you're an early riser too. By the way, you look great today! A.

Wait... Was this? Was he?

I read the e-mail again.

Yep. Aaron Taylor was flirting with me.

A smile bigger than the Macy's after-Christmas sale spread across my face. My mind raced. Wouldn't it be awesome to go out with this guy? I'd love to gaze into those gorgeous eyes across the table at a romantic restaurant. I'd love to spend a Saturday sailing with him on the lake.

Hold on, Patti. Don't jump off the deep end. Talk about a kamikaze move with your career. You've heard all those stories about office romances ending in disaster. If you get into a personal relationship with this guy, you can say good-bye to a future with this company.

Even though, for the right man, I'd give up my job in a New York minute, deep inside, I knew that Aaron was not the guy for me. Yes, he was handsome. He was successful. He was fun and easy to talk to. But I could tell he wasn't serious about a relationship with God. He didn't even go to church. He was out on the lake in his boat every Sunday.

My relationship with God was the most important thing to me. I needed a man who felt the same way. Years ago I had promised God that I would wait for a man with a heart for Him—a man with whom I could glorify God better than I could glorify Him alone.

But then again, Aaron was such an incredible catch—smart, good-looking, funny. I could spend years with him and never get bored. It was rare to find myself so attracted to a man and even rarer for the feeling to be mutual. Oh, I'd had a crush on Todd Simms from Bible study for the past four years, but Todd treated me like a little sister. I had admired Keith Dailey, my Sunday school teacher, since the first day I met him six months ago. But to Keith I was just another face in the crowd.

So here was Aaron—flirting with me—and, wow, was I ever attracted to him! I knew he wasn't a churchgoing guy, but what could I do? I certainly couldn't ignore his e-mail. I didn't want him to think I was rejecting him. That would make things terribly awkward.

Thank you so much, Aaron! I really enjoy chatting with you too.
Patti

There. Over and out. Okay, back to work.
I opened my file and tried to concentrate.
Bling.

Maybe some rainy Saturday when we're both running behind,
we'll find each other here slaving away at the office. A.

There was nothing I'd rather do than to spend a rainy Saturday with Aaron. But how was I supposed to respond to this one? I was so drawn to this man—but deep inside I knew I needed to end it right away.

Patti, just politely tell him no, and leave it at that.

But how could I tell him no when everything in me wanted to say yes? Maybe he really wanted to get serious about God but just didn't know how to do it. Maybe if he went to church with me a few times he'd realize what he'd been missing. Maybe all he needed was to spend some time with me and get a little spiritual encouragement. Besides, what if I hurt his feelings? What if he got mad at me and decided not to extend my contract? At the very least, it would be uncomfortable to see him every morning in the break room.

Patti, you'd be a fool to risk it with this guy!
Oh, what the heck.

Well, Aaron, there's an awfully good chance I'll see you here
some Saturday. I keep thinking I'm ahead of the game, and
then I end up with another pile of work on my desk! (Of course,
it sure is nice to be needed.) ☺ P.

There. Now he won't feel rejected, and I didn't commit to anything.
Oh please, Aaron, don't respond.
Bling.

I'll look forward to that Saturday, Patti. Hope you make it soon! A.

What do I do now? I have to say something. Oh, I know…

☺

There. That should do it.

I didn't get any more e-mails from Aaron that day, but all I
could think about for the next eight hours was gazing at him from
across the table at a candlelight dinner for two.

The next morning in the break room he was his usual charming self. But this time he reached over, touched my arm, and smiled
as he turned to walk back to his office.

My heart jumped, then melted. From that point on, I was
hooked.

That day Jenni gave me an offer to extend my contract another
six months. What an answer to prayer. I signed it and went home
that night a very happy woman. Maybe they'd offer me a perma-

nent position before the whole thing was through.

Another couple of weeks, another string of e-mails from Aaron—a little friendlier, a little more frequent. Then…

> Patti, maybe I'll see you on Saturday? I have to come in since I'll be out of town Thursday and Friday—nothing worse than starting Monday behind the eight ball! I'll be here about 1:00. (Just in case you were wondering…) ☺ A.

Oh, I've got to stop this! It isn't getting easier. I'd mentioned a few things about church when we were in the break room, but he wasn't very receptive. He wasn't serious about God, and worse yet, I worked for the guy! *This is a train wreck waiting to happen. Just level with him, Patti! You'll regret it if you don't.*

> Aaron, I've got to be honest—there's nothing I'd rather do. But I've been thinking a lot about this lately. I've got to step back. I can't get into a personal relationship with someone from work. Things just get too complicated. I really enjoy working here, and I'd hate to jeopardize our professional relationship. I hope you understand. P.

Okay, I told him. Plus, I let him know it wasn't anything personal. Surely, he won't feel rejected. Surely, he'll understand.

I tried to get back to work, but I couldn't stop thinking about watching the sunset on a warm summer evening with Aaron on his sailboat.

Bling.

Aaron's name flashed in the corner of my screen. As usual, my heart skipped a beat. How could he have this effect on me?

Patti, come on. It'll be fun. Don't worry about the work thing.
There's no way I could feel uncomfortable around you. We'll
have a great time together. A.

Wow! This guy was persistent—and it was so hard for me to
tell him no. Something about him drew me in. Something inside
me wanted him to want me. But that silent voice kept telling me
to run.

All the while another silent voice was trying to convince me,
"You only live once!"

Aaron, believe me. It won't be easy for me to stay away. P.

Send.
*Patti, why did you say that? You're only adding fuel to the fire!
Bling.*

Perfect answer! ☺ I'm on my way to the airport. I'll stop by and
see you in a minute. A.

My heart raced as I pretended to be hard at work. But all I
could think about was how Aaron's sky-blue eyes perfectly
matched the shirt he was wearing that day.

Within minutes he was in my office handing me a piece of
paper. "I'd like you to read this. I'll see you next week." He seemed
so businesslike.

Then he flashed that heart-stopping smile, winked, and was
gone.

He had scrawled his cell phone number across the paper. "Give
me a call if you get a chance. I'll miss seeing you in the morning. A."

I stared at the paper. I'd love a long chat with Aaron—time to talk when we didn't have to worry about someone walking into the break room or overhearing us in the office next door. Maybe, just maybe...

I carefully folded the paper and slipped it into my purse.

Bling.

You look great again today. A.

He'd sent it from his wireless. *This guy sure knows how to make a girl feel special.*

Thanks, Aaron. Have a wonderful trip and hurry back. I'll look forward to seeing you. P.

Patti, why are you encouraging him?

We're really going to have some great times together... Don't you agree? A.

Patti, don't go there!

I think there's an awfully good chance. ☺ P.

Do I hear an elusive yes? A.

Oh, Patti! Leave it alone! You're getting in over your head!

My, my, you ARE a closer! Yes, that would be a "yes." ☺ P.

We're going to be great together, Patti. Can't you tell? I'll bet
we devour each other given the first chance. What do you
think? A.

I stopped. I couldn't believe what I'd just read. What was he
saying?

You know exactly what he's saying.

But those weren't the words I wanted to read! That wasn't the
direction I wanted this to go. How could I respond to that? Would
he think I'd been leading him on? How could I get out of this one?

The craziest thing was that I really didn't want to.

I thought for a minute.

Well Aaron, you've actually done it. You've left a writer at a total
loss for words. Quite a talent you've got there! ☺ P.

Maybe he'd just back off. Maybe he'd realize I didn't want to go
there. But what in the world was wrong with me? Why did I still
want to go out with him? How could I be so drawn to a man who
was making it clear he had only one thing in mind?

But oh, how I loved to watch those blue eyes as they teased me
every morning. Oh, how I loved to see his name at the top of my
inbox. I loved to pretend I didn't notice him whenever he walked
by my door, but I had memorized the rhythm of his footsteps, and
my heart jumped every time he went by. I loved wondering which
dress he'd like best when I opened my closet each morning. I loved
wearing the shoes with the little higher heels because I caught him
looking at my legs once.

Oh, Patti! Please open your eyes!

Bling.

Don't be shy, now. Come on, babe. Step out.

The next line he wrote stopped me dead in my tracks. How could he send those words over company e-mail?

Ohhh, Aaron! I'm not sure what I'm stepping into. I guess I tend to be a slow mover. P.

Stop by on Saturday, Patti. You'll be glad you did. I'll miss you till then. A.

When I read his P.S. at the bottom, I was glad no one was there to see me blush.

After five months, he had finally laid it on the line. Unfortunately, it wasn't the line I wanted to hear. He hadn't even asked me out for dinner before going straight for the jugular. Part of me was angry.

But part of me wanted to take the bait.

What was I doing? This would lead nowhere—nowhere but trouble. But why didn't I put the brakes on in the beginning? Something inside had been telling me to stop. Why did I ignore it? Why did I keep going? Now I was in over my head. But I loved the feeling of drowning in Aaron! The longer I played this ridiculous game, the longer I wanted to play it

I opened a drawer and reached for a file. *Patti, don't waste your time thinking about him. You've got a deadline tomorrow.*

But I couldn't stop thinking about Aaron. He was everything I wanted in a man. Well, almost everything. Surely—eventually—I could change the rest. I was so attracted to him. He had a wonderful way of making me feel special. Men like Aaron didn't come around every day. What if I told him no and never found another?

Forget him, Patti! I opened a folder. Now where had I put those notes?

I longed to see Aaron on Saturday. We wouldn't get physical; we would just talk. Maybe we'd even talk about God.

Get real, Patti. You know better than that. You know if you see him on Saturday, you'll take one look at him and melt. Plus, you can't get into a relationship expecting him to change. You'd just be setting yourself up for heartache.

Where were those notes? Maybe I had put them in the file from Wednesday's meeting.

Think about it, Patti! Use your head. You and Aaron are on two different planets. He thinks sex before marriage is fine, but you know it's not. You've read about the consequences in your counseling classes. If you can't control yourself before you're married, it's hard to trust after you're married. And without trust you can't have real intimacy.

The price is too high, Patti! Don't even go there!

I knew the right thing to do. I also knew verse after verse that confirmed it.

For this is the will of God, your sanctification; that is, that you abstain from sexual immorality. (1 Thessalonians 4:3)

Beloved, I beseech you as aliens and exiles to abstain from the passions of the flesh that wage war against your soul. (1 Peter 2:11, RSV)

War against your soul. I sure knew what that felt like.

I also knew that the Bible said I need to marry a Christian—a man who believes in God the same way I do. A man with whom I could live a life that would matter in the end.

Do not be bound together with unbelievers; for what partnership have righteousness and lawlessness, or what fellowship has light with darkness? (2 Corinthians 6:14)

Even Solomon in all his wisdom was led astray by his unbelieving wives. Yes, I knew exactly what to do.

"RUN, PATTI, RUN!"

I knew it in my head, beyond a shadow of a doubt. But why wasn't the rest of me listening?

The battle was still raging by the time I'd finished work, made it through the evening, and crawled into bed that night.

As I stared up at the ceiling, I decided it was time to have another little chat with God.

Lord, I began, *I don't even want to pray—but I know that's when I need it most. I know what to do, but I don't want to do it. I'm headed for trouble and don't even care. I don't have the strength to win this battle. I'm tired of fighting. I want to give in!*

I forced myself to crawl out of bed and get down on my knees. Then I whispered a halfhearted prayer. *Lord, make me want Your will. Make me want to obey You.*

It was all I could muster.

Back in bed, I couldn't stop thinking about running my fingers through Aaron's velvet hair.

Finally, I sat up, turned on the light, and reached for my Bible. I didn't want to open it, but I knew I had to. It was my only hope. I had to get my thinking straight. I had to get my life back in line with God's will. Anything else would only end in disaster.

God, I know I'm playing with fire. After all these years of waiting, I don't want a man who will draw me away from You. I know that if I disobey, it will hurt my fellowship with You. You've told me: "If I regard wickedness in my heart, the Lord will not hear" (Psalm 66:18).

God, I want You to hear my voice, and I want to hear Yours too.

As I prayed, I was very aware that He was letting me make that choice. But I was afraid I wasn't strong enough to hold out for what I knew was right.

Rarely do I simply open the Bible and ask God to speak, but that night it was all I could do. I opened my Bible and began to read the first words I saw on the page.

> But, beloved, we are convinced of better things concerning you.... For God is not unjust so as to forget your work and the love which you have shown toward His name...[be] imitators of those who through faith and patience inherit the promises. For when God made the promise to Abraham, since He could swear by no one greater, He swore by Himself, saying, "I will surely bless you and I will surely multiply you." And so, having patiently waited, he obtained the promise. (Hebrews 6:9–15)

My eyes filled with tears. What a faithful God I serve. Again, He knew just what I needed—a gentle reminder of the blessings He gives to those who wait for Him.

> For from days of old they have not heard or perceived by ear, nor has the eye seen a God besides You, who acts in behalf of the one who waits for Him. (Isaiah 64:4)

Even though I had no doubt that God's words were true, I knew that without His help, I could never win this fight. I cried out, "Lord, do what it takes to keep me out of trouble! Discipline me! Take my life before You let me turn from You."

I lay back down with my Bible next to me and asked God to help me wait for a man who loved Him. Then, through my tears, I asked Him for rest.

Within minutes I was fast asleep.

9

the fight: the final round

▶ The swish of my raincoat echoed through the empty hallway.
Occasionally it paused as the click of a switch tossed a cascade
of light down the corridor in front of me.

I passed Aaron's darkened office and longed to hear his cheer-
ful greeting. Morning wasn't quite the same without his smile. My
heart was heavy with the memory of the prayer I'd prayed the night
before.

I'd better get used to mornings without Aaron.

I opened my office door and faced a stack of folders. A red light
on my telephone flashed. A few quick taps on just the right numbers, and I heard Aaron's voice on the recording. "Patti, it's ten
o'clock and we just finished dinner. I'm at the Ritz Carlton. I wish
you were here. I'd love to share this place with you."

Oh Aaron. Just the thought of being with him in an elegant place like the Ritz…

Hang on, Patti. You've got to be strong.

I booted up the computer and sat down at the keyboard.

Aaron, I just got your voice mail. I'd love to be there with you, but I have a feeling we're on two different pages. Can I call you tonight? I'd like to chat, if you have a minute. P.

Later that morning I got his response.

My meetings should be finished by 6:00. Call me anytime after that. A.

That night I dialed the number he'd scrawled across the page. "Aaron Taylor," he answered.

"Hi, Aaron Taylor. It's Patti Gordon."

"Well, hi, Patti Gordon!"

I loved to hear him say my name. *(Stop it, Patti.)* I asked about the meetings, and we chatted about his trip. Then I swallowed hard. "Aaron, I'm beginning to realize we're coming from two different places as far as a physical relationship goes. I don't believe that sex before marriage is right. Besides, I'm a strong Christian. I need to be with someone who believes the same way I do."

He listened intently, respectfully. He was kind and caring. He didn't even try to convince me that I was wrong. He said he understood. I hung up the phone, put my head in my hands, and thanked God that He'd made it so easy.

The next morning the coffee in the break room didn't taste

quite as good. I wondered what they were serving for breakfast at the Ritz.

I got to my desk and opened my inbox. There was an e-mail from Aaron!

Patti, let's try to find a middle ground. A.

Oh, Aaron... How can I stay away from him? *Patti, remember your prayer.*

Aaron, I know it's frustrating. But I've found it works best to face these things up front. It saves so much heartache in the end. P.

I didn't hear another word from him all day.

I hurried down the hallway to start another Monday. Aaron was supposed to be back today. I caught my breath when I saw the glowing light coming from his office.

Keep cool, Patti. He's just another coworker.

I paused in his doorway, "Good morning, Aaron."

He smiled. "Good morning, Patti." His crystal-blue eyes met mine. Suddenly, my world was at peace.

We had a nice chat as we waited for our coffee. I poured a cup then dashed off to meet with Jenni.

It was almost noon by the time I got back to my office and sat down to check my e-mail. Hmm. One from Aaron.

A reply would be nice. A.

What was he talking about? I scanned other e-mails that had arrived while I was gone. He'd sent another at ten o'clock.

Let me know what you think. A.

Had I missed something? I clicked Reply.

So sorry, Aaron. I didn't see that you had sent me anything. I was in a meeting with Jenni. Not sure what you mean, but I'll be over in a second. P.

I grabbed a pen and notebook then headed to Aaron's office.

The door was open. I knocked lightly. "Come on in." He looked up. "Close the door."

I stepped into his office and hesitantly pulled the door shut behind me.

He smiled, got up from his desk, and walked toward me without saying a word.

What was…?

He stopped in front of me, reached for my shoulders, then slid his hands down my arms.

I looked into his eyes. "What…?"

He touched my chin. "Come here," he whispered. Then he gently pulled me toward him and kissed me.

My mind was racing. What was happening? I pushed back, but he held on tight.

Then I melted.

But what was I doing? I was playing with fire. This guy wasn't right for me. Besides, I could lose my contract for this.

"Aaron, I…" I pushed my hands against his chest.

This time he drew back.

"But... What...? Why...?" I couldn't put two words together.

He held my face in his hands, looked into my eyes, and smiled. Then he turned and walked back to his desk.

I stumbled backward, opened the door, and left.

Thank heavens his secretary had already gone to lunch. I must have looked shell-shocked as I reeled down the hall.

Once inside my office, I closed the door and sat motionless. *What just happened? What did I just do?*

Oh, but I'd enjoyed it...way too much!

I sat for a minute to clear my head, then gathered my composure and tried to get back to work. I'd think about this tomorrow. Yes, that was it. Tomorrow I would know the right thing to do.

In the meantime, I opened my inbox. Wait! There was another e-mail from Aaron. He'd sent it early this morning—8:35—long before the others.

Patti, I'm still looking for that middle ground. How about this? Come down to my office and close the door behind you. Then I'll say "Good morning" the way I've wanted to say it since the first day I met you. I'll be waiting. A.

Oh no. He must think I got this e-mail.
I clicked reply.

Aaron, I just opened this one. When I came to your office, I hadn't seen it yet. I had no idea what you wanted to do. Oh Aaron, I'm so sorry. This will never work. We're just too different. It's such a fight for me (as I'm sure you can tell). But I

can't do this anymore. It's just too dangerous. I really enjoy
talking with you, but I can't get into anything else. P.

A moment later...

Patti, you're thinking too much. Let's just enjoy each other. A.

I closed my eyes. *Oh, Lord, please give me the strength to stay
away from him!*

But staying away from Aaron was not an easy assignment. It
had been ages since I'd felt this way. From the moment I opened
my eyes in the morning, all I could think about was Aaron. We had
so much fun whenever we talked. When I walked past his door,
everything in me wanted to stop. On Saturday afternoons it took
all my strength to stay away from the office.

Over the next few weeks, Aaron's e-mails kept coming. He
wasn't about to give up that easily.

Another Monday rolled around, and my resolve was running
thin. I hadn't seen Aaron since early that morning, and it was
almost time to call it a day.

Bling.

How about taking a look at some photos I took during my last
trip to Paris. Come on down if you've got a minute. A.

Patti, don't go there, I told myself. Then a verse came to mind.

No temptation has overtaken you but such as is common
to man; and God is faithful, who will not allow you to be
tempted beyond what you are able, but with the tempta-

tion will provide the way of escape also, so that you may be able to endure it. (1 Corinthians 10:13)

But, Lord, I don't want an escape right now!

I'll be right down. P.

Patti, don't do this! I reached in my purse, grabbed my compact, and peeked in the mirror. A dusting of powder, a swish of mascara, and I was off down the hall.

His door was open. I knocked and stepped inside.

"Hi," he said softly. "Close the door."

I did.

"Come on over. I've got them on the screen."

I was drawn like a moth to the flame.

"Come on around."

I circled his desk and stood next to his chair.

He began to explain the photos on the screen. The Eiffel Tower at night, a magnificent picture of the Arc de Triomphe. He reached for my hand and pulled me onto his lap. Then his gaze locked mine. "Patti, stop running from me."

I heard myself whisper, "I'm tired of running from you."

He leaned in and kissed me.

I was losing this battle, and I knew it. But then again maybe I could change him.

"Aaron," I whispered, our faces close. "Will you go to church with me?"

"Let me think about it, Patti." He ran his fingers through my hair and kissed me again.

This time I kissed him back and meant it. I slowly stood up

and smiled as his fingers lingered in my hair. Then I slipped down the hallway and back into my office.

I reached into my purse and peered into a tiny mirror. Thank heavens no one saw me. My hair was ruffled and my lipstick was gone. Anyone could have figured this one out.

Patti, one of these days, you're going to get caught. Someone's bound to see you leaving his office. It'll ruin your reputation, and that's not an easy fix. You know that "A good name is to be more desired than great wealth" (Proverbs 22:1).

You're playing Russian roulette, Patti! Someday you want to write a book about God. You can't do that if you're the kind of girl who fools around at the office! Plus, you've got to make a living. Your career depends on your reputation too.

There was no doubt that I had too much to lose. What a fool I was to risk it all on a few moments of pleasure.

Bling.

Patti, thank you. Let's do it, again…soon. A.

Aaron, you're a dangerous man! P.

Oh, maybe he'll change. Maybe he'll see the light. I struggled to focus on the file in front of me, but…

Bling.

Patti, I wanted to get back to you about church. I'm encouraged that you're trying to bridge the gap between us. But there's still another gap that will shut us down soon if we don't close it now.

I know your thoughts about sex before marriage, but as you
know, my view on sex is different. I don't see it as something
two people need to postpone until marriage. I wouldn't be
willing to wait for that with you (as I think you can tell). As far as
church goes, I've gone before, and at times it opens my eyes to
some things. But I live in a very intellectual world and am
comfortable with what I believe.

So if and when you are ready to play in my physical world, I'll
be ready to listen to your spiritual world. I'll understand if you
aren't willing to go there, but I just want to make sure you know
where I stand. Feel free to take as long as you need to think
about it. A.

I covered my face with my hands and sighed. Even my soul
seemed weary.

He couldn't have made it any clearer. I appreciated his honesty,
and there was no doubt what I needed to do. There was only one
problem—I had no willpower when I was around him. Worse yet,
it was impossible to put up a fight when I didn't even want to win.

I needed to end it. *Now.* But I saw Aaron every day, and he was
so persistent. How could I find the strength to stay away from him?

Then I remembered God's promise. He said He would provide
a way of escape. *Okay, Lord, I'm desperate. I'm taking You up on Your
promise. It's the only way I can get out of this mess. So where's the
escape, Lord? Do You want me to quit and find another job?*

My heart fell to my feet at the thought of it. I loved this company and everyone in it. There had to be another way. Maybe Jenni
would help me. She was a strong Christian. We shared the same

values and had become good friends. I could trust her to hold me accountable to stay away from Aaron. I'd already gone against my better judgment. I'd sat on his lap and kissed him at work! I'd already firmly established the fact that I couldn't trust myself.

That was it—I needed a backup. I knew Jenni would help me.

I slipped through the hallway and into her office. "Jenni, could you go to lunch today? There's something I'd like to talk to you about."

She looked up from her computer, puzzled by my tone. "Sure, how about one o'clock?"

"Thanks, Jenni. That'll be great. I'll come and get you."

She smiled. "I'll see you at one."

As we sat across the table, I told her everything. The chats every morning, the e-mails, the phone call, and even the kiss. I told her how hard it was for me to resist him.

Jenni's brow furrowed. She listened without interrupting. When I was finished she said, "Patti, I'm so concerned about you. Aaron is way out of line. You've told him no, and he needs to stay away. I know how hard it must be for you when you're so attracted to him. But I'll hold you accountable and help you any way I can."

"Thanks, Jenni. I knew I could count on you." The tension drained from my shoulders. What a relief just knowing that she would be watching out for me. Then we bowed our heads and prayed that God would give us strength and wisdom.

The next morning I arrived at work with a thermos of coffee in my hand. I had just booted up the computer and was pouring my first cup for the day when Jenni walked in and sat down.

"Patti." She looked awfully serious. "I'm sorry I have to tell you this, but I just reported Aaron to human resources."

"What?" I felt nauseous. She couldn't have said that.

"Last night I couldn't stop worrying about you." Jenni looked down as she continued. I could see that there were tears in her eyes. "I don't want you to be angry, but I had no choice. I have a responsibility as a manager. We have a sexual harassment policy. It says that if I know about anything like this, I have to report it to HR."

How could this be happening? I stared at my hands still clutching the coffee cup. I couldn't look Jenni in the eye.

"You work for him, Patti. He has power over you. I have to protect you and the company. If Aaron doesn't learn that this is inappropriate, someday we'll be hit with a sexual harassment lawsuit. Plus, I'd never forgive myself if something happened to you."

My stomach was churning.

Why hadn't I thought this one through? Of course she had a responsibility. Of course she had done the right thing. But in that moment I was angry at Jenni. Why didn't she talk to me before she reported him? I would have laid it on the line with Aaron. He never even got a warning. How could I face him again?

But deep inside I knew that Jenni had done exactly what she needed to do. Aaron was so persistent, and I didn't have the strength to resist him. Jenni knew it. I knew it too. She heard it in my voice. She saw it in my eyes. It was only a matter of time.

As much as I hated to admit it, Jenni was the answer to my prayer. I'd asked God to keep me out of trouble. Since I wouldn't obey Him, He let Jenni protect me instead.

Jenni was a friend in every sense of the word. She had done what a good friend would do—whatever it took to keep me on the straight and narrow, far away from sin.

"Patti," she continued. "There's one more thing. Aaron doesn't talk much about his personal life, but I casually asked his secretary yesterday afternoon."

I looked up at Jenni. Her eyes were still brimming with tears. Where was she going with this?

"Patti—" She hesitated. "Aaron is married."

Someone must have punched me in the stomach. I leaned forward with my face in my hands. "Oh, no."

"He's got three children."

I moaned. "Oh, Jenni, I had no idea." Through my hands I whispered, "How could he do that?" A tear dropped onto my lap.

Jenni came over and gave me a hug. "Patti, you didn't know."

True, I didn't know that Aaron was married. But that didn't erase the fact that I had ignored that silent voice that kept telling me to run. I had kissed the husband of another woman—the father of three children. I had flirted with him those mornings in the break room. I had talked with him much more than I should and laughed with him way too much. I flashed those smiles over my shoulder whenever I turned to walk out the door. There were so many times when I heard his voice then just "happened" to run into him on my way to get more coffee.

All along that silent voice had been telling me to stop. Why didn't I listen?

I hugged Jenni back. "Thanks, Jenni. I'll be all right."

But after she left I closed my door and cried for almost an hour.

The rest of the day was a nightmare. The human resources manager came by to talk. I told her that my relationship with Aaron had been consensual. She said that Aaron was still at fault. He was my boss and had power over me. Based on the e-mails, she could clearly see that he was pursuing, and I was pushing back. She said she didn't blame me.

Somehow that wasn't much comfort.

Aaron's boss had already been notified. Aaron would receive a written reprimand. I wasn't to speak with him about it at all.

After she left, I closed my door and had another good cry.

I saw Aaron in the hallway a couple hours later. He was as cold as ice. But I was angry too. What was he doing to his wife and three children? What had he tried to do to me?

That night I got down on my knees. *God, I'm sorry I ignored Your warnings. I chose to disobey You, and I don't want to do it again. Thank You for Jesus. Thank You that He died for me.* Then after I owned up to my part of the ordeal, I forgave Aaron for his part.

From that point on, when I was at work I hardly left my office. I didn't want to run into Aaron or his boss. What did his boss think of me now? He wasn't very friendly anymore. Did they tell him the whole story, or did he think that I was trying to break up a marriage?

Weeks crawled by. I couldn't concentrate at work, and I lay awake for hours every night. God had given me the job of my dreams, and I had turned it into a place of torment. Why had Aaron been so hard for me to resist? Had I played a role in ruining his marriage? When I disobeyed God, I always regretted it. Would I ever learn?

Even though those questions sawed at my soul, the thing that kept me up at night was the frightening realization of how weak I really was. I didn't have the strength to run from that battle. What would have happened if Jenni hadn't ended it? Now I could never write and speak about God. I couldn't be sure that I wouldn't dishonor His name.

I looked at the clock. It was almost midnight. Weeks had passed, and I couldn't let go. I hadn't had a decent night's sleep for quite a while. It looked like tonight would be no exception. I sighed, reached for the lamp, then groped under the bed for my Bible. Its pages had been catching a lot of teardrops these days. It fell opened to the book of Ephesians. I read:

> He chose us in Him before the foundation of the world, that we would be holy and blameless before Him. In love He predestined us to adoption as sons through Jesus Christ to Himself. (1:4–5)

More teardrops fell on the pages as I read those verses again and again.

God always gave me exactly what I needed, and this time I needed to be reminded that from the beginning He knew every sin I would ever commit. He knew that Aaron would tempt me and that I would ignore His warnings. Yet even then, He sacrificed His Son to make me holy and blameless.

But as I sat in bed with my Bible on my lap, I sure wasn't feeling very holy and blameless. I knew there'd be consequences for what I had done. Sin always takes its toll. But if I was so blameless, why was I so miserable?

Then I realized the battle wasn't over yet. There was still a final round of this fight that Satan was trying to win—the final round of guilt.

He was trying to convince me that if I was miserable enough, it would make up for what I had done. But no amount of misery had the power to do that. Only the blood of Jesus could cleanse me.

I knew it. Satan knew it too.

I crossed my arms and shook my head. Satan wasn't one to let the truth get in the way. He was determined to make me think that

I wasn't worthy of God's blessings. If he could get me to believe that God could never use me again, he could stop me from moving forward to serve God in the future. He was trying to steal my joy and contentment and keep me from glorifying God.

And I was doing an awfully good job of letting him.

So I crawled out of bed, got down on my knees, and thanked God for showing me the truth. Then I told Him that I was sorry. I had disobeyed Him by hanging on to guilt. I had chosen to listen to Satan's lies and had refused to believe Him when He said I was forgiven. Then I bowed my head and begged God to bring Aaron and his family to Jesus. I wanted them all to experience the peace and freedom I felt at that moment.

I cried for the umpteenth time that month, but this time they were tears of joy. The fight was finally over, and the final round was mine. And now I knew that the only power that guilt could have was the power I gave it, because Jesus had fought the final round and paid the ultimate price for me. So no matter how battle scarred I might be, no matter how weary my soul might become, no matter how many times I might grieve because I'd waved a white flag of surrender, Jesus would be there with both fists raised—waiting to hand me the victory. The only thing I had to do was take it.

He chose us in Him before the foundation of the world,
that we would be holy and blameless before Him.
In love He predestined us to adoption
as sons through Jesus Christ to Himself.
EPHESIANS 1:4–5

10

paradise

Two big brown eyes peered at me from above a pink powder puff.

No migrating mascara. Good.

I clenched my teeth, parted my lips, and inspected a line of pearly whites stretched across the miniature mirror. It had been ages since lunch, and I'd just brushed an hour ago, but you never know. Definitely worth a double (or was this a triple?) check.

I slid my fingers through the roots of my hair. *Maybe just a little more fluff.* Then I dusted the powder puff across my nose and forehead, skimmed rose-colored lipstick across my smile, clicked the compact shut, and slipped it into my purse—again.

My foot rocked a tiny tempo as I sat, legs crossed, on a chair outside the restaurant door. I folded my arms, unfolded my arms, tugged at my skirt, then fluffed my hair just one more time.

Where were they?

Wrought iron benches scattered across the patio were peppered with other hungry customers-to-be, all mercilessly teased by the sumptuous aromas drifting through the summer air. *Why did I get here so early?* Of course, I wanted to be here when they arrived, but I hadn't counted on the toll the summer heat would take on my now-glistening forehead and wilting white blouse. I wanted to look my best. After all, the last time I'd seen them was almost fifteen years ago.

It had been a beautiful day for a wedding at that little country church in Nebraska. Sean and Tracie were the picture-perfect couple—the kind you would expect to see standing on mounds of shimmering icing at the top of a tiered wedding cake. She was a gorgeous brunette with a Barbie-doll figure and a heart that loved the Lord. He was dashing with his dark wavy hair and bottomless brown eyes.

And there's something about a man in a tux…

It had been strangely surreal watching Tracie float up the aisle toward Sean's beaming smile. Almost two years earlier, I'd been planning to do the very same thing.

Sean and I had dated for almost a year. During that time we spent countless hours chatting over coffee on cold Nebraska days. Summertime brought picnics, water guns, and trips to the country. Passing months uncovered an abundance of shared interests, common goals, and growing love.

Sean wanted to serve God. I wanted the very same thing. We read books together, worked out together, loved the symphony together. Sean was everything on my list—from "loves Jesus" to "likes to slow dance." He told me I was his list too. He brought out the best in me. He said I did the same for him.

When he proposed, my answer was yes. Then off we went to look for rings. One setting after another slipped on and off my finger. Drops of sparkling diamonds on fields of black velvet flaunted their beauty under a tiny magnifying glass. But just as the diamonds under that lens grew to gigantic proportions, so my doubts and fears ballooned until they were all I could see.

Two weeks after we were engaged, I asked if we could wait awhile—back up a little—just to be sure. My fear and confusion puzzled me. I had no idea where it was coming from and no clue how to stop it.

After a couple of months, I finally assumed we just weren't meant to be.

The breakup was hard for both of us. We loved and respected each other. Above all, we were friends. But if we couldn't move forward, it was time to break up and move on with our lives.

Almost a year later the telephone rang, and my heart soared when I heard Sean's voice. He asked if I could meet him for coffee.

I reveled in the joy of being with Sean again as I watched ribbons of cream follow my circling spoon. He told me about his projects at work, his new dog Duke, and a Bible study he was leading. Then he told me about Tracie.

He didn't want me to hear the news from anybody else. He and Tracie had fallen in love and were beginning to talk about marriage.

My breath caught in my chest. My heart began to sink.

"Oh Sean," I said, "I'm so glad for you." *But why didn't I mean it?* I *wanted* to mean it. After all, I'd given him up long ago. He and I weren't meant to be. I'd tried, but just couldn't go there.

"Patti, she's wonderful," Sean said. "I think you'll really like her when you meet her."

"I have no doubt that I will." I looked him in the eyes and smiled. How could I be so confident on the outside when inside I really didn't want to meet Tracie...at least not yet? Of course she was wonderful. Sean was wonderful. Surely they'd make a great couple. Someday we'd all be fabulous friends—but *someday*, just not now. I wasn't ready for that.

Oh, why am I reacting this way?

I wanted Sean to be happy. He was an amazing man who would make a great husband and father. Sean wanted a wife and a family someday. He deserved to be happily married.

And, by golly, I was determined to be happy for both of them. I leaned forward with my elbows on the table, chin in my hand, and said, "Tell me more about her, Sean."

Then I listened.

As months passed, that sense of loss grew into acceptance and finally a sincere happiness for Sean and Tracie. Every now and then I'd run into them. We'd chat about the latest goings-on. Tracie was so good for Sean. It was clear that she adored him, and he seemed to bask in her admiring gaze.

Soon their wedding invitation arrived. Before long, I was sitting in that little country church, hankie in hand, watching them pledge their undying love.

After the wedding, Sean took a job in another state. Only Christmas letters brought news of their life together.

I went on to finish graduate school. Then I moved across the country, found a job, a wonderful church, and tried hard to find a husband. After all, marriage was my dream.

Each Christmas, another letter arrived from Sean and Tracie. They told of two growing girls, a new home, and summers full of fun and family vacations. It was the life Sean always wanted. The life I wanted too but could never quite have.

Ten years later I had still been wondering when it would be my turn to walk down the aisle. But what was holding me back? Was there a reason I couldn't commit to marriage?

I had gotten on my knees and had asked God to show me. He had led me to a promise I'd made after my father died: a promise to protect my heart. Then He had broken through the walls I had built, helped me overcome my fears, and opened my heart to love once more.

I thanked God for His answer to my prayer but wondered why He hadn't shown me sooner—soon enough to say yes to Sean and recognize that my uncertainty was nothing more than the fear of losing him. But that was a long time ago. Life had moved on. Sean was married, and I was finally ready to meet God's man for me.

One Saturday morning the telephone rang. A dear friend asked if I could come for a visit. Stephanie had just moved to the city where Sean and Tracie lived. Seconds after the receiver hit the cradle, I rummaged through my purse. After I picked through a dangerous assortment of pens and a small fortune in loose change, my hand emerged triumphantly unscathed, clinging to a tattered gray address book. Soon Sean's voice was on the line. He and Tracie could meet me for dinner. What a blessing it would be to see them again after all these years!

My stomach growled. I glanced at my watch. Seven o'clock. They should be here any minute.

I looked down at a tired white blouse and cringed at the rumpled spot left by my seat belt. Why hadn't I worn the blue sundress?

"Gordon!"

The voice was unmistakable. I'd almost forgotten. He called me by my last name whenever he wanted to tease me.

I sprang to my feet, whirled around, and fifteen years melted in an instant. It was Sean all right—handsome and confident, just the way I remembered him. The only evidence of the years that had passed were the fine lines etched at the corners of his eyes and the touches of gray splashed across his temples.

He smiled and hugged me tight, just like an old friend would. "Tracie's working late. She should be here soon," he said. "Let's go ahead and get a table."

The hostess led us to a corner booth in the dimly lit restaurant. Soft light trickled from the lamp above as Sean asked about my mom and sisters. I asked about Tracie and the girls. We talked about work and ministry, laughed about old memories, and inquired about old friends.

Sitting across from him was so comfortable, so familiar. He seemed at ease with himself and his world. He'd found his dream and was living it fully. He'd become the man I always knew he would be: a leader, a giver, a caring man who never stopped growing.

Our conversation was delightful, its rhythm eerily familiar. I sensed when he would turn a phrase or when a joke was coming. He voiced my thoughts before I spoke. He knew just when to speak and when to listen. We laughed at the same things, questioned the same things, enjoyed the same things. Nothing had changed—or so it seemed.

Only now he was happily married with two wonderful daughters. And I was still single with a medley of memories and a long string of heartaches behind me. As we sat together in a booth in the corner and stories from the past unfolded, a lifetime of relationships brought perspective and confirmation to the dawning realization that Sean was the rarest of treasures.

It was Sean who drew me in, Sean who made my world stand still. It was Sean who dreamed the dreams I wanted to help come true. That was the moment I realized that it was Sean I'd been searching for these last fifteen years.

I drew a sharp breath.

Sean spoke, but suddenly I didn't want to listen. I didn't want to face the flood of memories his voice awakened.

I wanted to forget about our kitchen capers: laughing at black-crusted chicken or puzzling over a flat soufflé. I wanted to forget about our fireside chats, our reading to each other on rainy days, or the times we had prayed together and both of us cried.

I didn't want to laugh with him or gaze into the eyes that had mesmerized me years ago. I didn't want to hear the voice that had whispered "I love you" and "Will you marry me?" I couldn't bear to see the arms that had encircled me so tenderly or look upon the hands that had held my face.

I didn't want to think about all the things that "might have been" or peer into a life that I could never share. All I could see was what a fool I'd been, and all I could do was pray that God would help me. Sean must not know about the war inside me. He belonged to someone else, and now that was God's perfect will for him.

And for me.

A beautiful brunette walked up to the table. Sean stood up and gave her a kiss; then she slid in beside him. Stunning as ever, Tracie hadn't changed a bit.

The rest of the evening I focused my attention on Tracie. She was the woman who had chosen to say yes and had stood bravely in her commitment. She was the woman who encouraged Sean, comforted him, and helped him become the man he was today. She was the woman who had suffered with him when times were hard, who shared his dreams and sorrows. She was his joy, his love, his life. She was that woman…because she had chosen wisely.

The evening passed. I smiled. I listened. I did my level best to hide the battle that would not surrender. Finally, it was time to go. We hugged good-bye, and they were gone—back into the world they'd made together.

And I was all alone.

Again.

I started the engine and began the drive back to Stephanie's. Darkness hid the tears that I could not.

How could I have been so blind? I could have been the one sitting next to Sean. I could have been the one gazing at him with loving eyes, holding his hand underneath the table. How could I have let a senseless fear rob me of that?

Fifteen years of hoping, praying, and longing for a husband haunted me. Those years never had to be. They were my choice, a foolish choice birthed out of fear—a fear of pain brought on by the death of my father. That fear had stolen Sean—the man that I loved. That fear had ruined my dreams. That fear…

Then it hit me.

That fear was not my fault.

I was only fifteen! I was in anguish. I didn't have a clue what I was doing. That promise I'd made to protect my heart was the only way I thought I could survive—the only way to shield myself from more hurt than I knew how to handle.

I was the victim of a tragedy over which I had no control.

And God could have changed it all.

Yes, God could have stopped the rain that day or slowed the car before it reached that mountain pass. He could have held my father and sisters safe within His arms—even in the midst of twisted metal. He could have spared their lives, but instead He stole them away. All the while He knew the love those wounds would steal from me.

My anger burned as tears rolled down my cheeks and fell to my withered white blouse.

But even if He had to take Dad and my sisters, He still could have let me have Sean. He could have opened up my eyes. He could have lifted that veil of pain so that I could see the love I'd been denying.

He chose the pain. He chose the sorrow. He chose a lonely life for me.

I chose paradise for you.

I froze.

They came from nowhere. Simple words filled with so much love that they pierced my aching heart.

But I could not—*would not*—listen. Why should I? This God did not play fair.

His silent words resounded. *I chose paradise for you.*

I was hurt and angry. I tried to ignore Him. I tried to silence the truth that echoed in my heart.

But I could not.

Little by little, those silent words slipped into my soul. My heart began to soften. Then, I conceded.

Yes, You did *choose paradise for me...*
and perfect love...
and perfect peace.

I opened the glove box, grabbed a tissue, and brushed a tear from my cheek.

How could I have missed it? In the beginning, God gave us paradise. He also gave His perfect love. But He didn't force us to love Him in return. He let us choose to love Him...or not.

And we did not.

Instead, we chose to disobey, and with that choice came death and sorrow. No, God did not destroy our paradise.

We did. By turning from the only One who could sustain it.

Dad and my two sisters were victims of a fallen world, treasures that were stolen by the choice of all mankind.

I couldn't deny it. Pain was not His choice. God was not to blame.

But even so, I drove into the velvet night, alone.

Morning peeked between the curtains. Exhausted, I stared at the ceiling. I rolled over and stared at the silhouette of an old rocking chair.

It had been a fitful night.

Tossing. Turning. Wanting to remember, yet wanting to forget.

How could I forgive myself for being such a fool?

More questions battered my heart: Why did God take my family when He knew how it would wound me? Why did He let me harbor those fears? Why did He let me pay such a price for something that wasn't my fault?

The morning sun began to awaken the yellow walls around me. Now I could see the tiny flowers on the sheets I'd pulled up to my chin. After a long and restless night, I had to find peace—somewhere. So I begged for the answer to one final question: "God, why did You allow it?"

For the same reason I made the blind man blind.

My brow furrowed.

I "heard" it, but what did it mean?

I knew the story of the blind man. His disciples asked Jesus why

God made him blind. Jesus told them, "So that the works of God might be displayed in him" (John 9:3). Then Jesus healed him.

"Yes, Lord, but…"

Then it dawned on me. God took away the blind man's sight for a few short years on earth. When Jesus healed him, God was glorified. In exchange for His glory, God gives rewards that will last forever. For the first time, I realized what God had done for the blind man. He took a finite investment and gave an infinite return.

And that was what God was doing for me.

He allowed me to be wounded so that He could use those wounds to glorify Himself. In return, He would give me rewards that would never fade away. Even though I couldn't see exactly how He was doing it, God was leveraging my life on earth for my greatest good in the end. A finite investment for an infinite return. For that I should be grateful.

I climbed out of bed, got on my knees, and thanked God for His answer. Yet I had to admit that, as I knelt, my heart still felt heavy. Someday I would have rewards in heaven, yet at that moment, heaven seemed a million miles away.

Then two verses came to mind.

I would have despaired unless I had believed that I would see the goodness of the Lord in the land of the living. (Psalm 27:13)

Do not call to mind the former things, or ponder things of the past. Behold, I will do something new, now it will spring forth; will you not be aware of it? I will even make a roadway in the wilderness, rivers in the desert. (Isaiah 43:18–19)

As I knelt by that bed and pondered those verses, the sorrow in my heart began to disappear. God, in His love and mercy, was planting seeds of hope for today. No, He didn't promise paradise on earth. He didn't even promise that life would be easy. He simply let me know that I would see His goodness in this land of the living, and He would give me a future if I would let go of the past.

I lifted my eyes. It was time to move forward, time to grasp the loving hand of the God of new beginnings. So I bowed my head, laid my love for Sean behind me, and closed the door to a past that I could never change. Then I reached over, opened the curtains, and let a new day pour into the room—a day of roadways in the wilderness and rivers in the desert, a day of hope and trust in a God who promised something new.

Do not call to mind the former things, or ponder things of the past.
Behold, I will do something new, now it will spring forth;
will you not be aware of it?
I will even make a roadway in the wilderness,
rivers in the desert.
ISAIAH 43:18–19

the masterpiece

▶ I bent toward a shimmering web of ebony spilling from a cardboard box.

Closer…closer…

What could it be?

I pulled the enticing textile until it dangled freely from my outstretched arm.

Hmm. Another mystery.

The house was full of them. Treasures from who knows where, purchased for who knows how much. But this one was particularly enchanting.

I gingerly lifted another edge to reveal a wisp of sheer black netting. Golden threads gathered one end. Graceful sashes danced around the other.

Its elegance was evident, but what in the world was it? Maybe some kind of cape?

I strolled to the mirror, pulled the gathers over my head, and peeked through the hedge of black ruffles that covered my nose. The sinuous sashes swirled around my blue plastic flip-flops.

Definitely not a cape.

I tilted my head and pondered yet another way to twist it, turn it, or tie it. How could I discover the secret of its form?

A swish of long blond hair flashed across the mirror as a giggling Rebecca bounded from behind. "Oh Patti!" She tried to contain herself. "That's a skirt I bought from a designer in Paris!"

I felt like the little country bumpkin who had just been caught, red-handed, drinking from the finger bowl.

She stifled her giggles and helped me emerge from yet another row of flowing ruffles.

"The gathers go at the bottom." She pulled it over her head. "You wear black tights underneath and tie the sashes around your waist." In the twinkling of an eye, the sheer shapeless wonder was transformed into a swath of elegance draped around her body.

"These shoes go with it."

Her hand disappeared into another cardboard box and reappeared holding the most treacherous pair of stiletto heels I had ever seen. As she slipped them on, I could just imagine my stunning friend stepping out into the Paris nightlife. She must have taken the breath away from every man in the room.

Rebecca gazed at her reflection and shook her head, lost in some faraway memory. "I won't even tell you how much I paid for it."

I sighed as I too shook my head.

Then as quickly as she had appeared, she shed the black wonder, handed it to me with a brilliant smile, and dashed off to help another clueless soul.

I continued my adventure through a field of open boxes stretched across the cavernous bedroom, the alleged skirt draped over my arm. Racks of colorful attire lined the walls. Piles of shoes huddled under a row of beaded evening dresses. Business suits, ski wear, pants, tops, dresses, boots...

I was surrounded.

I had no idea that one human being could own so many clothes. The rest of the house mirrored the same marvel. Masses of luxurious furniture and lavish accessories throughout—each with its own scarlet price tag.

I had known Rebecca for less than a year, but for months before we met, her story had echoed through conversations with my friends and acquaintances. Its twists and turns continued to unfold as we wandered through its remnants. Her story transfixed us all as we watched it dance on the line between riches and ruin.

Years ago, Rebecca had gone to college for an MRS degree. Four years later, she posed for pictures with a tassel on her cap, a diploma in her hand, and no diamond ring on her finger.

The wild and crazy coed had tried her best to catch a man, but the hook came up empty every time. Although she was sure that a husband would bring happiness, if she couldn't get a man to bite, she'd find happiness somewhere else. The almighty dollar was the next stop on her list. If there was even a bit of bliss in that dollar bill, Rebecca was determined to find it. Besides, a little cash might be just the bait she needed to catch herself a man. So she dreamed up a business, worked night and day, and made money hand over fist.

Before long, her burgeoning bank account was begging for relief, so she bought a Jaguar...then a Porsche...then a 6700-square-foot home, complete with its own swimming pool and tennis court—in the middle of one of Atlanta's most prestigious neighborhoods.

Rebecca was finally happy. For a couple of weeks. But hanging on to happiness proved to be as tricky as holding the smoke from her last cigarette.

Maybe money wasn't the ticket after all.

So what about friends? Surely a bunch of friends would make her happy. The magazines and movies said they would. Plus, while she was out searching for friends, she'd double her efforts to find a husband. So the gorgeous (and now wealthy) Rebecca invaded the Atlanta nightclub scene looking for love and friendship.

When Rebecca worked, she worked hard; when she spent money, she charged full force; and when she partied, she did it with reckless abandon. Thursday, Friday, and Saturday nights she hit the bars only to return for another spree on Sunday afternoon. Sometimes she blacked out. Some mornings she swore that she would never drink again. But she'd be back that afternoon searching for relief from another hangover.

By the time she was thirty-six, Rebecca had spent ten years at the bars dating scores of men and meeting countless people. But she never found the happiness those magazines and movies promised. She did everything they said to do and bought everything they said to buy, but life didn't turn out the way they said it would.

It finally dawned on her that someone had lied.

To complicate matters, over the next few years, the economy in Atlanta began to take a turn. The river of money that had poured into her business suddenly slowed to a trickle. If that wasn't enough, Rebecca began to uncover some secrets about her incredible home. Her house was what you might call an "impulse buy." She saw it, she loved it, she bought it—lock, stock, and barrel—without an inspection.

But Rebecca had gotten a "bonus" along with her real estate deal.

The house came complete with a truckload of termites and a list of structural problems longer than her bleached blond hair. Builder after builder told her it would cost more to fix the place than it was worth. Her best bet was to tear it down and build another. But with business bottoming out, Rebecca couldn't afford to build a new house. And she couldn't even sell the house for what she still owed.

She was trapped—without love or money, in a house that would eventually fall down around her.

Rebecca had reached the end of the line. She'd tried everything she could try, bought everything she could buy, and knew more people than she could shake a stick at. But the beautiful, wealthy, perfectly dressed Rebecca had few real friends, no love, and very little happiness. Now she was convinced that nothing—absolutely nothing—could ever fill that hollow, empty feeling in her heart, so she did the only thing left to do.

She gave up.

Rebecca spent the next year alone in her palatial prison. She went weeks without seeing another human being. She worked long hours conducting her business over the phone and spent nights and weekends crying on the sofa while she smoked, drank, and watched TV.

Suicide began to look like the only real solution. How would she do it? When would she do it? How long would it take before someone found her body? Who would even miss her? Certainly not her family—she hadn't spoken to her own father in over twenty years.

As thoughts of suicide twisted through Rebecca's mind, something else began to haunt her—a Bible study she'd heard about over a year ago. One of Atlanta's megachurches hosted it every Tuesday night. Three thousand singles attended each week.

For months she ignored the thought. Why would anyone, much less a bunch of singles, want to study the Bible? That was at the very bottom of the list of things Rebecca wanted to do. Yet, for some reason, she couldn't quit thinking about it.

Finally, out of curiosity (and maybe just a glimmer of hope that she would find her man), she cleaned up, dressed up, and showed up one Tuesday night in March.

The doors opened, and Rebecca strode into a massive auditorium. Row after row of countless blue chairs stretched like an ocean before her. Some were filled with singles lost in conversation. Others held the belongings of someone hurrying across the room or chatting with a friend in the middle of an aisle. Thousands of conversations blended into a buzz that floated through the flurry of activity.

Rebecca surveyed the crowd. Some people looked like they were still in college. Others had been out for a good long while. Some were dressed in suits, others in jeans and T-shirts. She saw diamond bracelets and expensive leather handbags, baseball caps, tattoos, and nose rings. What a strange mix of humanity. But the strangest thing of all was that every single one of them seemed to be sober.

Go figure.

An enormous stage stretched across the front of the auditorium. Above it hung a gigantic banner with a peculiar message:

Thou art great, O LORD God: for there is none like thee, neither is there any God beside thee, according to all that we have heard with our ears. (2 Samuel 7:22, KJV)

How odd.

Rebecca had never read anything like it. Yet the words that seemed so foreign imparted a strange sense of peace—an unfamiliar feeling to a girl who'd spent the last week trying to decide between razor blades and an overdose. Puzzled, she wandered down an aisle and perched hesitantly on an empty seat.

Musicians took their place on stage and began to play. Aisles emptied as rows of chairs were transformed into a sea of singles. The music swelled. The crowd rose to its feet and sang along with words that appeared on screens beside the stage. They were words Rebecca had never heard before—words about God, words about His love, words that stirred a tiny ray of hope still buried in her heart.

She bowed her head and watched teardrops disappear into the toes of her black suede shoes.

The music ended, and a man stepped on stage. He talked about people who didn't feel loved by their fathers. He told of their struggle to feel worthy of their heavenly Father's love.

Rebecca bowed her head again and watched those tiny teardrops fall. Strange, oh so strange, how that message touched her.

The next Sunday she awoke early and drove back to the auditorium. Another man spoke, and again, she wept. What drew her to this place?

Week after week she returned.

Then one Tuesday night, Rebecca heard something she'd never heard before. The man who spoke said no one was perfect. Every one of us had sinned.

Rebecca had no doubt of that. Her conscience had told her many times that what she was doing was wrong.

He said that sin is like a cup of sewage in a pitcher of water. No matter how much sugar we add, it will never make the water pure.

No matter how many good things we do, we can never erase the sins we've committed. We can never make ourselves perfect. On top of that, the Bible says that God can't let an imperfect person into a perfect heaven.

Rebecca had never heard that before. In fact, she'd always heard that if she was good enough she would go to heaven. But deep inside she always wondered: how good was "good enough"?

The man kept talking, and things got worse. Since God is a God of justice, He can't ignore our disobedience. So He said He'd allow a sacrifice to cleanse us from our sin. But since God can't accept imperfection, the sacrifice had to be perfect. Unfortunately, nothing on earth was perfect—we'd all made sure of that. Without a perfect sacrifice to cleanse us...

Every one of us was destined to hell.

Rebecca started wishing she'd never come to Bible study. From what this guy was saying, she would never be happy—not even after she died. In fact, hell sounded a whole lot worse than what she was going through now. Her last bit of hope was sinking fast.

But then the man opened the Bible. He said that because God loves us, He gave us all a second chance. In His infinite love and mercy, He provided His own perfect sacrifice. He sent His Son to die for our sins. "For God so loved the world, that He gave His only begotten Son, that whoever believes in Him shall not perish, but have eternal life" (John 3:16).

The man went on. The Bible says that good works are still important. Once we are in heaven, we'll be rewarded for them. But faith in Jesus is the only thing that will actually get us there. "For by grace you have been saved through faith; and that not of your-selves, it is the gift of God; not as a result of works, so that no one may boast" (Ephesians 2:8–9).

Only faith in Jesus can save us. Jesus said: "I am the way, and the truth, and the life; no one comes to the Father but through Me" (John 14:6).

Rebecca sat spellbound. She had never heard anything like this before. It all seemed so simple. It made so much sense. But what was the next step? What should she do?

As if to answer, the man continued. All God asks is that we believe in Jesus. But God requires more than an intellectual belief because: "The demons also believe, and shudder" (James 2:19).

The original Greek word the Bible uses for *believe* means to "trust and commit." The kind of belief that God requires of us is to trust and commit our lives to Jesus.

Then the man asked everyone who wanted the gift of eternal life to pray a prayer along with him.

Rebecca bowed her head.

"Lord Jesus," he began, "I want to know You personally. Thank You for dying on the cross for my sins. I open my heart and receive You as my personal Lord and Savior. Thank You for forgiving my sins and giving me eternal life. Please take control of my life, and make me the kind of person You want me to be."

Rebecca prayed that prayer that night, and oh, how she meant it. Then an amazing thing happened.

Nothing she had ever done before had truly satisfied. Yet as she prayed that prayer, her heart was filled to overflowing with what she'd longed for, what she'd searched for: peace, *perfect peace*.

This time, her tears were tears of joy.

As months unfolded, Rebecca's newfound faith seeped into every corner of her life. She bought a Bible and began to read. Its truths drew her into an intimacy with God she had never imagined existed. It challenged her to a life of obedience and surrender to His will.

Sunday mornings and Tuesday nights brought new friends for Rebecca—friends like none she'd ever known. They prayed with her, laughed with her, and opened up their hearts to share her joys and struggles. These were the friendships she'd ached for— open, honest, satisfying, centered in a love the world could never give.

Then one Sunday morning as she sat in the auditorium, the speaker started talking about a mission trip to Asia. Millions of people there had never heard of Jesus. A group from church was going. Rebecca sensed a gentle tug to join them.

Weeks passed, and that gentle tug continued. She thought about her years of searching. How could she refuse to go when others must be searching too? How could she keep silent when millions would perish without Jesus? Where would she be now if someone had not shared with her?

Weeks later, Rebecca stepped off a plane halfway around the world. She seemed so different from the people of that country. She was tall; they were small. Her hair was blond; theirs was black. But as she gazed into each smiling face, she sensed a heart like hers—a heart that longed for peace and ached for the contentment that only Jesus gives. As she told the Asian women about Jesus, she watched them give their hearts to Him, and they too shed tears of joy.

Rebecca returned to the United States, but the tug toward Asia would not go away. In fact, it grew, fueled by a loving force she could not resist. She wanted the Asian people to know Jesus more than she'd ever wanted anything else.

Even more than she'd wanted marriage.

But a foolish decision she'd made years ago still hung like a noose around her neck. She was trapped in a glittering façade with an arrogant address. Why in the world had she bought that house? But try as she might, there was no breaking free. She had painted herself into a corner.

But Rebecca kept reading her Bible and believing that what it said was true: "Nothing will be impossible with God" (Luke 1:37).

She served a God of miracles. He healed the sick. He raised the dead. If that same God was calling her to Asia, surely He would find a way to sell her house so she could go.

So she decided to trust Him.

She learned about a ministry in Asia and signed up to join them in less than a year. Then she planted a "For Sale" sign in the middle of her yard...

And waited.

That's when I met Rebecca. And we waited together.

We met for coffee, shared stories of our lives, and prayed.

As months flew by, she raised money for support and even made plans to give her business to a friend. But that pesky "For Sale" sign would not surrender its place in the middle of her yard.

So we prayed...and waited...and the deadline for Asia drew near.

Ten weeks and counting. The telephone rang. Rebecca was crying. What should she do? It was time to buy her ticket to Asia—almost two thousand dollars—an awful lot of money for Rebecca these days. But she couldn't go to Asia if she didn't sell her home. Her missionary's salary for an entire three months wouldn't cover a single mortgage payment.

So we got together with a bunch of our friends and prayed for wisdom for Rebecca.

She bought the ticket.

Eight weeks and counting. It was time to get rid of some

things. Rebecca's house was packed with furniture and all kinds of expensive belongings. But Rebecca couldn't take them with her, and she wasn't sure she would ever come back. This would be the biggest garage sale most of us had ever seen.

But Rebecca had a dilemma on her hands. Shouldn't she sell the house first? Everyone knows a house sells faster if it's fully furnished and beautifully decorated. Then again, if she waited much longer, she wouldn't have time to get rid of her things.

But what would she do if she couldn't sell the house and she'd sold or given away everything in it?

Those were questions none of us could answer.

So Rebecca prayed. Then she called the newspaper and placed an ad for a four-weekend-long garage sale.

The next month was a whirling blur of sorting, pricing, and watching strangers with fists full of twenties carry Rebecca's possessions away. All the while, the "For Sale" sign taunted us from its throne in the middle of the yard.

I continued to wander through that bargain-hunter's paradise, then peered into a box of sweaters and grabbed three turtlenecks off the top. They were just my size and colors. Ninety-dollar price tags still hung from the sleeves. The garage sale tags said five.

Sold.

My arms were loaded—blouses, boots, sweaters, skirts. *Enough already!* It had been a tough year financially, and even though I was surrounded by countless boxes of undiscovered bargains, I had to cut it off somewhere.

I picked a path through the bedroom, found my way back down the stairs, and ambled into the disheveled living room. It was the fourth and final weekend of the sale—only an hour to go.

It looked as if the entire place had been ransacked by an army. Truckloads of goods had already been sold, but piles of items remained. Christmas decorations, a couple of lamps in the corner, a set of dishes—the list went on and on. In an hour we would be closing up shop, getting the good stuff ready for consignment, and hauling trunks full of leftovers to the Salvation Army.

Rebecca and a handful of other weary friends had plopped themselves down on whatever was seat-worthy. I paid for my plunder then took my place on an empty stool next to her.

A few last-minute customers still strolled around the room. Occasionally, a new one meandered through the open door. A middle-aged couple picked up a tennis racket, paid for it, and left.

I peeked at Rebecca out of the corner of my eye. Her face was tired and pensive, but smiling.

"What are you thinking?" I asked.

"I wonder what God will do next," she replied. "I've done everything I can. Now it's up to Him."

If only that stubborn "For Sale" sign would budge. But it didn't look good at the moment. Four more weeks to sell a home that no one had bid on for almost a year? What were the chances? In a month, would Rebecca be on a plane bound for Asia—or sitting alone in an empty living room?

If I was a betting woman, I wouldn't put my money on the plane.

"No telling what He'll do," I said. "But whatever it is, it'll be what glorifies Him most."

"I know that's right." She smiled that tired smile again. "And I really believe it means that, somehow, He'll get me to Asia."

We all admired Rebecca so much. She was convinced that God

was calling her to share Jesus with the people of Asia. Now she was giving up everything she owned to answer that call from Him. Rebecca was so sure that God would do a miracle.

As for me, I had no doubt that God could do it. He had the power to do anything. But as much as I'd hoped and prayed for Rebecca, I had to admit that I wondered. *Would He?*

Would He rescue her from all her mistakes—from the years she'd made poor choices and spent money like water? Would He intervene and sell the house she bought without an inspection? Rebecca had changed in so many ways after she gave her life to Jesus, but she'd made an awful lot of mistakes in her life. Was it too much to ask God to erase the damage she'd done? After all, He didn't owe her a thing.

I'd wondered about that many times—not about Rebecca's life, but about my own. I too had made mistakes in the past and lived with the consequences day after day. I'd made foolish decisions in dating, investments, career choices, friendships. You name it. And even though I knew I was forgiven, I still had so many regrets.

A customer leaned down and rummaged through an open box. I glanced at my watch—ten minutes till six. The marathon was almost over.

"Hi there!" A voice called from the entryway. I looked toward the door to see a familiar face. It was a woman who had been here with her husband a little while ago. All they had bought was a tennis racket. She was looking straight at Rebecca. "Have I got a story for you!"

"Can't wait to hear it!" Rebecca said as she stood up.

The woman walked toward Rebecca and continued, "After my husband and I went back to the car, I couldn't get your house off my mind. I saw that it was for sale, but we already own a beautiful home. It doesn't make sense to buy another one."

"Of course it does!" Rebecca laughed as she tossed her head.

"Our kids are leaving for college. We need a smaller house—not a bigger one. So we both agreed that we wouldn't even think about it. Then we drove on to find the next garage sale."

Rebecca smiled and listened intently.

"But the strangest thing happened. A few minutes later, we found ourselves back in front of your house! We have no idea how we got here! So I thought I might as well come on in and take a closer look around."

"That's the best story I've heard all day," Rebecca said as she laughed again. Then she led the woman to the basement to show her the termites and structural damage.

I sat on that stool and wondered what God was up to this time. Rebecca had to sell the house for at least what she owed—an impossible price and an impossible deadline. Only God could pull this one off.

So I closed my eyes and asked God for a miracle. Then I thanked Him for my precious friend—a friend who believed Him for impossible things, a friend who trusted Him to take her mistakes and use them for His glory.

And He did.

The woman and her husband both loved Jesus. They sensed He was leading them to buy Rebecca's home. Three weeks later they closed on the house. The following week, I gave Rebecca a hug and watched her walk toward a plane bound for Asia. Through tears of parting, I couldn't help but smile for the joy of a priceless lesson.

God used Rebecca to teach us all that He can take our broken lives and transform them for His glory. "He will give beauty for ashes, joy instead of mourning, praise instead of despair. For the LORD has planted them like strong graceful oaks for His own glory" (Isaiah 61:3, NLT).

He loves to give us beauty for ashes. He longs to redeem us from the things we have done—if we will only let Him. He wants to use our faith and obedience as the canvas on which to paint a master-piece—a masterpiece that clearly displays His mercy and compassion—a masterpiece that shows the world that there is no fail-ure, mistake, or sin that He cannot use for His glory and our good.

As the years go by, I continue to receive letters and e-mails from Rebecca in Asia. She tells about adventures and joys in her life, about trials and pain God uses to refine her. She shares about miracles she has seen and Asian men and women who have come to know Jesus.

Each letter reveals another glimpse of the masterpiece God continues to unfold—a life changed, a hope renewed, another rela-tionship mended. He wants us all to reflect His glory from every facet of our lives, to experience the beauty that accompanies sur-render—to join Him in accomplishing something greater than we can comprehend. Yes, He wants us all to be a part of His magnifi-cent masterpiece. All He asks from us is the canvas of a life that is yielded to Him.

He will give beauty for ashes, joy instead of mourning,
praise instead of despair.
For the LORD has planted them
like strong and graceful oaks for His own glory.
ISAIAH 61:3, NLT

section

4

finding the
▶ lover
of your soul

There is a God-shaped vacuum in the heart of each man
which cannot be satisfied by any created thing,
but only by God the Creator, made known through Jesus Christ.

BLAISE PASCAL

We are *made* to depend on God;
we are made for union with him
and nothing about us works right without it.

JOHN ELDREDGE, *WILD AT HEART*

Do not look for God to come in a particular way,
but *look for Him.*

OSWALD CHAMBERS
MY UTMOST FOR HIS HIGHEST DAILY DEVOTIONAL

the good life

▶ The beams of the headlights slipped along the side of a blue sedan then returned their frozen stare from the reflection in my neighbor's window. Thank heavens for a parking spot close to my apartment. I was glad I wouldn't have to end a long, hard day hauling bags of groceries up a hill.

The engine stopped. The lights went black. I sat for a moment in silence.

It felt great to get out of the apartment—even if only for a quick trip to the grocery store. It was 8:00 P.M. before I had realized there was no milk for tomorrow's breakfast. And there was nothing for dinner except the crusted edges of a week-old lasagna I'd left in the refrigerator because I didn't have time to wash the pan.

Grocery shopping had been the highlight of my day. I'd spent the first ten hours sitting in a closet. Although my apartment was far from a feature in *Southern Living*, it did have its redeeming qualities. A favorite was the second walk-in closet in the bedroom. My wardrobe fit easily into closet number one. That left closet number two as the likely candidate for a home office.

It was just big enough to lay part of an old tabletop across a couple of two-drawer filing cabinets. A tattered green office chair, given to me by a merciful neighbor, filled every inch of the remaining space. If I tucked the printer under the desk and was careful not to stretch my legs, I was ready to make a living.

I'd been working hard and had finally landed my first technical writing contract. The deadlines were straight from an ivory tower. And the pay…? Well, let's just say that I'd need quite a pitching arm to hit market rate from here. But it was money and, more importantly, a chance to get some experience.

I pulled the key from the ignition and reached for my purse.

Up to this point, my writing career had swung wildly between feast and famine. Even during the good times I was afraid to spend money since I never knew for sure if I'd have work tomorrow. Technical writing contracts lasted six months to a year. If I could get some experience, it might open the door to a steady income down the road.

But this contract was turning out to be a little tougher than I'd planned. The software I was documenting was so unstable that my computer crashed more often than the cars in a demolition derby. And the developers who were supposed to explain how the software worked were so busy trying to smooth out the kinks that they didn't have time to answer my questions. Plus, they were in Denmark—a visit to the office to bribe them with cookies was simply out of the question.

So I sat in my closet, day after day, knocking my head against those tiny little walls and trying to figure out what had happened to my data. To complicate things, I hadn't seen a healthy paycheck for quite a while. After I had finished my last writing project, the company I worked for said they didn't have the money to pay me. So along with a closet full of technical difficulties, I had a few budget problems to boot.

How could someone who worked so hard be so broke?

I reached over and grabbed three bags of groceries then began the trek to my front door. My stomach growled, and my head was starting to hurt. Cracks in the sidewalk reminded me that these apartments were over twenty years old and not known for their stellar upkeep. It had taken management two whole days to fix the upstairs neighbor's pipes, which had rained an ocean in the middle of my living room. After something with a good set of teeth had gotten into my storage closet and chewed through a box of Christmas decorations, I was determined not to renew my lease. But after days of pounding the streets looking for another place, it soon became apparent that this was all I could afford.

My stomach roared again. It was way past dinnertime. That gallon of milk was getting awfully heavy, and there were three more bags of groceries in the car.

As I lumbered along I thought about how different this was from the life I'd planned. I wasn't supposed to be this poor. I wasn't supposed to spend my days sitting in a closet. I didn't need to be rich, but I wanted to have a few nice things. If only I had a bigger income, I could buy a new sofa in any color I wanted. I wouldn't have to settle for someone else's castaway sitting in the driveway at a neighborhood garage sale. If only I had some money in the bank, I could go to the theater or symphony. If only I had a little extra cash, maybe I could take a vacation.

If only...

I always tried to keep an eye on the sunny side of life, but here I was—in the middle of reality with an empty stomach and an aching head—trudging up the steps to a run-down apartment with a big brown stain in the center of the ceiling.

Why wouldn't God answer my prayers? Maybe He wanted me poor. But I wasn't about to let that happen. I had big dreams for my future, and I might have even found a way to help a few of them come true! Yep. There was finally a glimmer of hope on the horizon.

Just over a year ago, a friend had told me about an investment. It was making him money hand over fist, so I had scraped together every penny I could find. I needed a miracle.

So far I hadn't been disappointed.

Within a few months, my money doubled—then tripled. Then it doubled and tripled again. I didn't have a lot to start with, but each month I scrimped and saved and mailed in another check. The thought of my growing portfolio always lifted my spirits. It was my big chance to get some nice things. Maybe I could even retire before I hit fifty!

I turned my key and pushed the creaky door open. I nudged the light switch upward with my elbow, hoisted bulging bags onto the counter, then headed back to get the rest of the groceries and the mail.

A little aluminum door swung open, and I grabbed a pile of junk-mail flyers. Nestled in the middle was a smattering of envelopes. I muttered a quick prayer that no bills would be due before my next paycheck, then thumbed through the envelopes to see what had arrived: a ministry newsletter, a bill from the electric company, another credit card offer (why were these crazy people wasting stamps on me?). I smiled. There it was—the quarterly statement for my investment.

My finger slid inside the flap, and I wrestled the statement from

its ragged edge. The paper unfolded, and the street lamp illuminated tiny numbers at the bottom of the page. I shook my head in
amazement as I calculated the giant leap the total had made in
three short months. I sighed, slipped the statement back into the
envelope, and decided that something with a fireplace in the mas-
ter bedroom would be nice.

I leaned down and grabbed the bags of groceries sitting at my
feet. As I lifted them off of the ground, they didn't seem so heavy
anymore! Yes, life was looking pretty good again. Everyone had stories of tough times they'd been through. I'd sure have great tales
about the days when *I* was poor. Thank heavens, those days were
almost over! Before long I'd be sitting on a luxurious sofa right in
the middle of my own living room. No more neighbor's leaky
pipes. No more cracks in the sidewalks. All my hard work was
beginning to pay off.

As I floated up the run-down steps, that silent voice surprised
me with a visit. *Pull your money out of that investment.*

I paused midstep. Why would I want to do that? I tried to
ignore it and reached for the doorknob.

Pull your money out.

But that didn't make any sense at all! Why would I toss aside
my only hope—the best thing that had happened to me since I
could remember? If I pulled out now, it would ruin everything. I
would never get out of this apartment. This deal was my only
chance. The returns on my meager mutual funds were trickling in
like a Chinese water torture. And if I kept all my money (what little
I had) in the bank, I would never have enough to retire.

I stepped into my apartment and locked the door behind me.

Southwestern Chicken… That might be good tonight. I began to
unpack the rest of the groceries. The microwave hummed, and a

spicy aroma filtered through the air. All the while my mind wrestled with that nagging notion.

Pull your money out.

No matter how hard I tried to concentrate on what I needed to do tomorrow or how many calories I'd eaten that day, that preposterous idea kept trying its best to yank me back to the poorhouse.

I thought about how many times I'd begged to hear that silent voice speak to my heart with comfort or direction. Instead, silence. Now it came from out of nowhere—completely uninvited—insisting on something I didn't want to hear. Certainly God had better things to do than tell me what to do with my money. Why couldn't He stick with things that really mattered—like world peace or feeding the hungry? Besides, I'd been praying for a decent income for years, but He just didn't seem to care.

Then a verse came to mind:

For the LORD God is a sun and shield; the LORD gives grace and glory; no good thing does He withhold from those who walk uprightly. (Psalm 84:11)

Yes, that verse was in the Bible, but it wasn't very easy to believe right now. I'd been trying to walk uprightly for an awfully long time, but some of those "good things" never seemed to materialize. How about a husband? How about a car without an oil leak? How about a job I enjoyed? If my life was what God called "good," then He and I weren't speaking the same language.

The microwave beeped. I felt like a hypocrite when I sat down to say the blessing. But God knew I was just trying to take care of myself so no one else would have to. Besides, He knew I'd give part of that money to the church or even some mission field out there.

I picked up my fork to take a bite.

Pull your money out.

I was getting tired of this! "Lord," I began, my patience wearing thin, "I know You're asking me to get out of this investment, but I don't want to be poor anymore. I want to do it my way—just this once. Jesus died on the cross for my sins, so I'll repent…later. But right now my answer is no. I will not pull my money out."

It was that quick, that simple, that honest.

The silent voice was gone, and I was free.

The beams of the headlights slipped along the side of a white sedan then returned their frozen stare from the reflection in my neighbor's window. Thank heavens for a parking spot close to my apartment. I was glad I wouldn't have to end a long, hard day hauling bags of groceries up a hill.

The engine stopped, and I reached over to grab three plastic grocery bags and a six-pack of diet soda. Maybe I could get it all in one trip.

February had come and gone leaving memories of another uneventful Valentine's Day. The sun was beginning to linger. The days were shedding their winter chill. The impossible project was over, and the bottomless pile of paper was gone. The project had been rough, and I knew I'd never want to do it again, but all the pain had been worth it. The experience had opened the door to another technical writing contract. This time the deadlines were reasonable and the pay rate was looking pretty good.

I grabbed the groceries and lugged them toward a row of mailboxes. A little aluminum door swung open, and I grabbed a pile of junk-mail flyers. Nestled in the middle was a smattering of envelopes. I muttered a quick prayer that no bills would be due before my next paycheck then thumbed through the envelopes to see what had arrived—an insurance bill, a wedding invitation, another credit card offer (why were those crazy people wasting stamps on me?). Then I smiled. There it was—the quarterly statement for my investment.

My finger slid inside the flap, and I wrestled the statement from its ragged edge. The paper unfolded, and the street lamp illuminated tiny numbers at the bottom of the page.

I blinked hard.

This couldn't be right. There had to be a mistake. This must be somebody else's statement. But I looked at the top of the page. There it was—my name and address, just as big as you please.

But where was all the money from last quarter? Where were those thousands of dollars? I stared at the paper in shocked disbelief as my dreams vanished into thin air.

I stood for a moment, unable to move, then numbly bent down and picked up the groceries. I plodded up the steps to my run-down apartment with a big brown stain in the center of the ceiling.

The bulging bags slid onto the kitchen counter then I trudged to the bedroom and lay, facedown, on the bed. *What happened? How can this be? Where did all that money go? How could it have disappeared so fast?*

I turned over and stared at the ceiling.

He had tried to warn me. He had tried to tell me. Why in the world didn't I listen? Why didn't I believe that He wanted what was good for me? Why couldn't I believe that He might want what I wanted too?

As I lay on that bed, I thought about so many other times I had ignored His voice—that tug of my conscience, those silent whispers, even the verses He brought to mind. Once I had accepted a job offer despite the silent voice that had clearly told me no. Sure enough, it had ended up being pretty miserable. Then there was Aaron Taylor. What a mess that had turned out to be! One by one, my mind went down a long list of examples.

Whenever I disobeyed God, I *always* regretted it in the end.

There was no denying it. God had never withheld anything from me—at least anything that was good. As I thought about the past, hindsight confirmed that He saw a bigger picture than my finite eyes could see. Only *He* saw the future. Only *He* knew the hearts of men. Only *He* had the foresight and wisdom to know what would and would not be "good" in the end. "For the LORD God is a sun and shield; the LORD gives grace and glory; no good thing does He withhold from those who walk uprightly" (Psalm 84:11, NASB).

Now I could see the truth of that verse from a brand-new perspective. It gave me a lens through which to see so many "good" things in my life. If He had given more money than I needed, I wouldn't have seen Him miraculously provide. If He had given me a husband at twenty, I might have taken him for granted. If He had given me everything I wanted, I might not have compassion for the poor.

I turned over on my stomach and propped up on my elbows. *So if I walk uprightly and don't have something now, it simply means it isn't "good" for me now.* God knows the past, present, and future, and He has every resource in the universe at His disposal. He's told me that He loves me and that He'll never forsake me. I can rest assured that He's provided what's best for me.

I sat upright and looked around a room filled with blessings. Then I climbed out of bed and headed toward the kitchen. It was time to unpack the rest of the groceries and fix something to eat. My hand reached into a plastic bag and pulled out three cans of tuna. For years tuna was all I could afford, but I smiled as I realized that was probably why these jeans still fit. Heaven help me if I'd had enough money to support a chocolate cheesecake habit. I gazed at the brown stain in the middle of the ceiling. That ordeal gave me a chance to make a lot of friends at the property management company. I looked down at my ringless left hand. Well…I'd just have to trust Him on that one.

Then a ragged envelope on the counter caught my eye, and I smiled as I remembered that I could.

The LORD God is a sun and shield;
the LORD gives grace and glory;
no good thing does He withhold
from those who walk uprightly.
PSALM 84:11, NASB

13

the deal

My chilly toes waded down carpeted stairs then touched the satin bareness of a shiny wooden floor. They padded past a chenille sofa, across an itchy rug, and up to my reflection in a darkened windowpane.

Beyond the window, a wintry world awaited. The sun had long since retired for the evening. The moon stood its careful watch as silent rays glimmered through branches of a leafless tree.

No sign of life outdoors.

The bluster of a January evening had emptied the streets of even the most avid exercise enthusiasts. Cars huddled in garages while children sat at dinner tables laden with bowls of steaming chili or plates full of macaroni and cheese. Glowing windows of the neighborhood reminded me that there was life beyond these walls.

For the past few weeks, I'd needed that reminder over and over again.

A pair of empty eyes reflected from the window. Lately, they'd been peering at me from every mirror I passed.

Lord, I miss my friends. Why are You making me spend all this time alone?

I'd asked that question many times, but never got an answer.

Lord, You know it's hard for me.

He was being awfully quiet.

I couldn't understand why He'd done this. I'd been begging Him to change things for almost a month. But the only thing that ever changed was the increasing number of hours I cried.

Those hollow eyes continued to stare. *Could I have changed things? Could I have made it turn out differently?*

I pondered for a moment. The answer was no.

Five years ago God had begun to bless my career more than I'd ever dreamed. I had picked up a technical writing project, then started another in instructional design. Before I knew it, companies were calling with more work than I could handle. After a couple of years I bought my dream home and began to fill it with all kinds of beautiful things.

Then the economy in Atlanta turned south, and I knew that consulting was not a safe haven. One of my clients offered me a job, so I jumped on board just in time. But the security of that job was short-lived. After a year, layoffs began, and I with half my coworkers poured onto the streets in the middle of the worst job market any of us had ever seen.

That was two months ago.

Oh, I knew how to pinch pennies—I'd done it most of my life—but now I had a mortgage payment due every month and friends who'd been out of work for almost a year. Not a promising combination. So I prayed, picked up the telephone, and two weeks later had a contract offer from one of the biggest companies in town.

My knees hit the floor, and I thanked God. Then I signed my John Hancock without a second thought.

In a decent market, I never would have even considered that contract. But from what I could see, it was the only game in town. The deadlines were ridiculous, and I had to work from home. The deadlines didn't worry me much—but the "home" part was a different story.

You see, I didn't like being alone.

God made me a people person. Too much time alone wasn't much fun for me, so I always found ways to be around people. When I started my business and worked out of my closet, I hit the gym every day. I'd stop and chat with the people who worked there. I knew their dogs' names, who they were dating, and where they went on vacation. Sometimes I stopped by the frozen yogurt shop and visited with the college kids who worked behind the counter. I knew all about their problems with roommates, the classes they were taking, and how they planned to spend the summer.

I love people—plain and simple—and when I was with them, I loved life.

But this new set of deadlines did not allow the luxury of seeing real people every day. Each morning I got up before the crack of dawn, opened my laptop, and worked until bedtime. Then I hit the sheets exhausted, dreading tomorrow's rerun.

Saturdays were filled with paying bills and catching up around the house. The best part of the day was a trip to the grocery store. Moms and little children wandered through the aisles. The checkout people even smiled and chatted a little. The grocery store was my big chance to reconnect with the world.

Sundays were my favorite days—going to church and spending

time with friends. But Sunday meant Monday was coming, with five more days of solitary confinement.

The whole time that I was miserable, I knew I should be thankful. At least I lived indoors and had plenty of food in the refrigerator. Besides, I knew I was never alone—God was always with me.

But if God was there, why couldn't I feel Him? Why was I still so lonely?

Oh, sometimes I sensed Him, but He wasn't like another human being. At times I "heard" His silent voice, but He never held a conversation with me or shared popcorn at the movies. He certainly never gave me a hug. I knew He was more than an imaginary friend, but why did the room still feel empty?

I looked out again at the neighbors' glowing windows then closed my eyes tight. "God," I began, "You know I need people. You *made* me that way. So please take away that need for them, or do something to fill it."

That prayer hit heaven with all the fervor I could muster. I opened my eyes—but nothing had changed.

I sighed, turned, and walked away from the empty eyes in the window.

My feet padded across the hardwood floor and up the carpeted stairs. Then I slid my chilly toes underneath a pile of blankets.

God and I counted the hours until morning.

BUUUZZZZZZ...

I reached over and hit the snooze button, determined to hunker down and let the world pass by. Sleep had been little more than a few fitful hours of tossing and turning that night. But a looming deadline dragged me to the starting line of yet another day.

As I cradled my morning cup of coffee, a glance at the calendar made my lonely heart leap. I'd forgotten I'd made plans to see Carolyn that evening! We'd talked about it over a month ago. She was finishing work on her PhD, and I was thrilled that despite her hectic schedule she was still taking time to get together with me.

But I had a set of files due tomorrow morning. Should I call and reschedule? But Carolyn was so busy. It would be hard to sync up our schedules again. And I really wanted to see her tonight. She was so much fun and was always so encouraging.

What the heck.

I was desperate. My mental health was on the line. I might not get much sleep tonight, but I'd find some way to get it all done.

I called and left a message. "Carolyn. It's Patti—just wanted to make sure we're still on for tonight. I'll be there at seven unless I hear from you."

I put down the phone and booted up my computer.

I couldn't wait to see her!

The hours crept by. Words crawled across the screen. The stripes of sky between the window blinds turned a brilliant blue…then gray…then black. Finally it was time to get together with my friend!

Lights along the freeway raced past my car windows as I marveled at the novelty of life outside four walls. It seemed like ages since I'd been on the road to anything other than church or the grocery store. I pulled into a parking spot in front of Carolyn's apartment, climbed the stairs, and knocked on her green door.

Her beaming face appeared. "Hi Patti! I'm so glad you could make it."

She gave me a hug, then invited me in for a nice hot cup of

coffee. There was so much to catch up on—work, school, our lack of social lives! Finally the conversation turned—as it always did—to the lessons God was teaching.

I told her about something that had challenged me recently. I'd heard a radio interview with Bill Bright, the founder of Campus Crusade for Christ. Bill and his wife, Vonette, had signed a contract almost fifty years ago to be God's slaves. They had surrendered their own agendas and pledged to live lives of obedience to Him. God used their lives, and now Campus Crusade is the world's largest Christian ministry, with staff in almost two hundred countries.

"Carolyn," I said, "that interview challenged me to completely surrender my life to God. I've been praying about signing a contract too. But this is serious stuff. I wouldn't dare make a promise to God without thinking it all the way through."

Then I shared a verse with her that I'd memorized years ago. "You shall be careful to perform what goes out from your lips, just as you have voluntarily vowed to the LORD your God, what you have promised" (Deuteronomy 23:23).

"Carolyn," I said. "I want to learn to trust Him in everything."

She looked at me. "I know what you're talking about, Patti. He's challenging me to trust Him too. He's been putting it on my heart to let Him wake me in the morning."

I opened my mouth to speak but couldn't think of anything to say. *What did she just tell me?*

Carolyn picked up her coffee cup and took a sip. "The hardest time was the night before my written comprehensive exams. They covered everything I had studied in my PhD program. If I didn't pass that test, I wouldn't graduate."

I was astonished at how the rubber met the road in Carolyn's relationship with God. She'd been working hard for the past three years and had finished most of her classes. Now she was telling me that she had risked her PhD if God didn't wake her in time to take the test!

"I was up late studying the night before and was so tempted to set my alarm. But I knew God wanted me to trust Him. So I did."

I squirmed in my chair. This was getting more uncomfortable by the minute.

Carolyn smiled. "Sure enough, He got me up and I passed with flying colors!" Her eyes were gleaming, as big as saucers, but not half as big as her smile.

I sat in that chair—leaning forward, coffee cup in hand, smiling on the outside, but stunned deep down inside. Somehow my mind couldn't connect the dots on this one. I admired Carolyn's faith, but I couldn't imagine putting something like that on the line.

Carolyn continued, "God's never let me oversleep—not once since I've asked Him to wake me. And that was over a month ago."

Her words hung in the air. Then I felt a gentle tug, a sense that God was asking me to let Him wake me too.

Now hold on a minute! I thought. I had files due at 9:00 A.M. It was already 10:00 P.M., and I hadn't even left Carolyn's. The drive home would take me at least half an hour. If I slept past 4:00, I'd surely miss my deadline. If I missed a deadline, I might lose my contract—and work wasn't easy to come by these days.

And that wasn't even the half of it! If I was out of work, I couldn't pay the mortgage. Then I'd lose my home.

Forget it!

The evening raced on as I tried to ignore that persistent, gentle tug. The next time I looked at my watch it was eleven o'clock—

way past bedtime. We both had full days ahead. I gave Carolyn a hug, stepped into the night, and closed the green door behind me.

A silent whisper echoed in the stillness.

Trust Me to wake you in the morning.

Suddenly I regretted ever praying to hear the voice of Jesus.

That silent voice spoke deep in my heart, that gentle tug pulled at me. I'd been around long enough to have a pretty good idea that this was the real thing. But there was one last ray of hope that I might be mistaken. Whenever I sensed that God might be speaking, I always put it through the acid test:

Does it contradict anything written in the Bible?

If it did, I knew for sure that it was not the voice of God. The Bible says that God doesn't change. He would never go against His written Word.

I got into the car and tried my hardest to think of a verse that contradicted those silent words.

I couldn't think of a single one.

Bummer.

In fact, the only verse that came to mind was, "Blessed is the man who trusts in the LORD" (Jeremiah 17:7).

Now, where was a good Bible verse when I needed it? Plus, the whole idea of letting Him wake me up didn't make a bit of sense. *That alone* had to count for something! I cranked up the radio, drowned out that whisper, and sang the whole way home.

Once in bed, I reached over and set the alarm for 4:00 A.M. It would be a short night, but tomorrow was Friday. Surely, I could survive on caffeine for one more day.

My head hit the pillow. I stared at the ceiling. Somehow my eyes just wouldn't stay shut. That gentle tug persisted and would not let me go. It was midnight now—four hours and counting—

I needed sleep to think clearly tomorrow. I didn't have time to toss and turn tonight.

Forty-nine, fifty, fifty-one, fifty-two... The sheep kept jumping, but my eyes stayed wide open. Then I tried to think about relaxing on the beach somewhere. I strained to hear the waves and feel the warm sand in my toes, but my mind kept drifting back to Carolyn's story.

Finally, I reached over and flipped the switch on the alarm to OFF.

Okay, God, You win. But if I miss my deadline and lose this contract please *find me another one.*

Within minutes I was fast asleep.

Bam! Bam! Bam!

What was going on? My groggy mind fought to grasp a single strand of consciousness.

Bam! Bam! Bam!

Who was pounding at my door?

Bam! Bam! Bam!

I struggled through the haze to reach a waking world. My eyes opened.

Suddenly, all was quiet.

"What was...?" My misty mind began to clear.

Darkness...stillness... No one was pounding at my door. I leaned forward to listen.

Absolutely nothing.

What just happened? What was that all about? I glanced at glowing numbers:

4:00 A.M.

The dusk of dreamland finally disappeared as I realized the pounding was only in my sleep. Then I remembered Carolyn's smile, her faith, her wisdom. A gentle tug, a silent whisper, the flip of a switch to OFF.

Then I remembered: "Blessed is the man who trusts in the Lord."

I tilted my head back and stared at the ceiling. A tear slipped down my cheek…then another…and another…

What had just happened? What had just gone on? The God of the universe had heard my cry—the God who had billions of important things to do. He kept the earth spinning and the stars burning bright. He kept the ocean churning and the hearts of billions beating.

Yet right in the middle of all of those important things, He humbled Himself to wake me up at exactly the time I needed. The God of the universe was there, while I slept, watching the clock for me.

I looked again at those glowing numbers. Sure enough, right on the money.

Then a strange thing happened as I sat on my bed. I noticed that the room wasn't empty anymore. God had asked me to give Him a chance to show me He was real—to trust Him and watch Him be faithful, to reach for His hand so He could grasp mine, to cast myself upon Him so I could feel Him catch me. Here I was— in His loving arms—sensing His presence in a way I never had before.

I thought about the years I'd prayed for intimacy with Him but didn't know how to find it. Now I knew that He would be as real as I would let Him be. If I would only obey Him, He would do miracles to reveal Himself to me. Tears rolled down my cheeks as I thanked Him for teaching me another priceless lesson: intimacy with Him is found in obedience and surrender.

I basked in His presence and wept.

Then I crawled out of bed, opened my laptop, and began to type:

My Pledge

On this day, I, Patricia Ann Gordon, solemnly give myself as a slave to You—God, the Father; Jesus Christ, the Son; the Holy Spirit; the Triune God; the Creator of all things.

From this day forward, I give all that I am completely to You for Your use and Your glory. I pledge to You my abilities, my talents, my time—all that I own and will ever own. I surrender my longings, my dreams, and my life. I will go where You lead me. I will do what You ask, whenever You ask. I fully surrender myself to You.

Only one thing I ask—that You teach me Your voice, that I may not be led astray by the voice of another.

It was a very simple prayer—every word of surrender that I could think of that morning. I printed it, got on my knees, and swallowed hard as I acknowledged that my life would no longer be my own.

Then I sensed the tender love of the God who was beside me and signed my name to the best deal that I have ever made.

"Blessed is the man who trusts in the Lord."
JEREMIAH 17:7

14

whole in one

"Oh, I'd love to!" I grabbed the electric bill, the only piece of paper within arm's reach, then snatched a pen and scribbled "January 27—6:00 P.M." on a blank spot next to the customer service number.

"You'll send directions? Thanks so much, Lorraine. I can't wait to see you!"

The dial tone hummed as I stared at the phone and wondered what I'd gotten myself into this time.

But what else could I do? It was obviously another open door.

I shook my head and marveled at how those doors kept opening. Who could have guessed that a dear friend from college would call and ask me to walk through another?

Lorraine and I had met at the beginning of our freshman year. I had gone through rush before classes began and found a home at the Tri Delta house. Every Monday the girls in the house were to get together for dinner and a meeting. It was our first Monday night—the day after rush—and time to meet the rest of my pledge class.

The front door of the massive house loomed in front of me. Would I fit in? Did I really belong? It was too late to turn back now.

I mustered my courage, opened the door, and stepped into a cloud of perfume. Elegant dresses, pretty lace blouses. I was surrounded by beautiful women.

I'd never been all that confident about the way I looked. Growing up, I was always the girl in class who was a little too tall and a little too skinny. My bangs were too short, my voice was too low, and my nose was a little too wide. As I got older and started filling out, I was sure that God had made a mistake. He'd obviously put the wrong top on the bottom. Eventually I learned to work with it, but I was always aware of my shortcomings.

There I stood, surrounded by a pack of perfect women. Gorgeous figures, beautiful hair, stylish makeup, manicures. Their chic couture could have filled the pages of a fashion magazine! I looked down at the best dress I owned, thought about the jeans in my closet, and wondered how I'd pull it off next week. My identity crisis was just getting on a roll when I noticed a stunning blonde standing next to me. She must have stepped right off the silver screen.

Her skin was flawless. She had long golden locks, and if I could've chosen a figure, it would've been hers. Her meticulous makeup and fashionable clothes made her look like she was waiting for a photo shoot. She was more than a bit intimidating to a homespun brunette who had never quite figured out what to do with her hair.

She smiled at me. I smiled in return.

"Hi, I'm Lorraine." She offered her hand.

I shook her hand and wondered how I'd keep the conversation

going. After all, someone that perfect had to be incredibly shallow.

But I was in for the surprise of my life. Lorraine turned out to be the highlight of my evening. She was so easy to talk to. In fact, we connected on so many levels. On the inside we had lots of things in common, but on the outside we were amazingly different. Lorraine was a vivacious blonde—always on the social scene. I was a people person too, but ended up spending most of my weekends trying to keep up with my classes. Lorraine loved to write. I hated to write. She loved public speaking. I'd rather take a beating. But Lorraine loved Jesus, and with Him as our bond, we became fast friends and roommates.

After college Lorraine moved away, but three years later, I sewed a rose-colored dress and walked down the aisle as a bridesmaid at her wedding. Even though we were half a country apart, we still kept in touch, some years better than others. It didn't surprise me when I learned that Lorraine had signed a contract to write her first book.

After the book, Lorraine began to speak at Christian women's conferences. About a thousand women attended each conference. There was always an afternoon session for singles.

So there I stood, staring at the phone, wondering what I'd say at her conference in Atlanta. Lorraine had just asked me to be on the afternoon discussion panel. Even though I was still a bit nervous about getting up in front of people, public speaking was not the biggest challenge with this one. This time it was the subject.

Sex.

Lorraine Pintus and Linda Dillow wrote *Intimate Issues,* a book on what the Bible says about sex and marriage. Their following book, *Gift-Wrapped by God,* is all about sex and singleness.

What was *I* going to say about sex to all those single women?

Thank goodness it's only the first of December, I thought. The conference was almost two months away. Surely I could figure out something by then. In the meantime, I would focus on trying to enjoy another Christmas season.

Yes, Christmas as a single was always a bit of a challenge for me. Everything about the holiday seems to revolve around couples and family. There are cute little kids singing Christmas carols dressed up like Joseph and Mary. Then there are all those TV commercials with great ideas about what to get my husband. Of course, it wouldn't be Christmas without the commercials to remind me that diamonds are forever.

Mistletoe in my house was like the hammer in my basement— you could've bet the farm that neither one would see much action this year. *Miracle on 34th Street* was another Christmas tradition, but if I had to watch it one more time, someone would have to talk me off the ledges. *Why don't those kinds of happy endings ever happen to me?* And after Christmas I still had to make it through another New Year's Eve. Who was going to kiss me to welcome in the New Year?

Oh, I tried to make the best of it. In fact, I'd made lots of wonderful Christmas memories. But I'd come to accept it as another fact of life: the holidays shone a spotlight on that empty place in my heart. Yes, somewhere in my heart there had always been a longing—a hollow feeling that nothing seemed to fill. The odd part was, I wasn't exactly sure what I was longing for. Was it for a husband, a family of my own, or maybe another Christmas with Dad?

All I knew was that during the rest of the year, I was better at covering up that longing. I stayed busy with activities and kept my social calendar full. But even though I packed my life with all kinds of wonderful things, nothing ever completely filled that empty place in my heart.

This year I decided that I would face the holiday season head on. I threw myself into decorating, parties, and shopping for friends and family. Christmas came and Christmas went. Then New Year's Eve was finally over. Down came the Christmas tree and all the fancy lights. Out went the thank-you notes, and another year was well underway. Business began to pick up again. Before I knew it, the conference was a week away.

I'd put it off for as long as I could. It was time to get my head in the game.

I knew that sex and singleness was an important topic. I had my struggles like everyone else. But I'd found, through the years, that dancing on the line was the surest way to a heartache. First, it shut down my fellowship with God. On top of that, it blinded me to important things about a man. When I was kissing him, I didn't really care if he had a little problem with lying. I also found myself ignoring the fact that he couldn't hold his temper in traffic. Somehow, all those red flags about things that make or break a marriage didn't seem to matter much when I was in his arms.

Yes, sex was a serious topic for singles, and I wanted to be prepared. First, I would read Lorraine and Linda's book. *Gift-Wrapped by God* had been patiently waiting on my nightstand for almost two months. With Christmas over, I finally had time to read a couple of chapters each evening. The book would give me a framework of ideas. I could take it from there.

So that was the plan until I sensed that silent voice.

I want you to fast and pray.

That had to be my imagination. Fasting just wasn't my thing. I knew the purpose of fasting—to deny yourself food so that you can focus on God. I'd done it before, but frankly I'd decided that there had to be a better way. I hated that gnawing feeling in my stomach. I hated all those hunger pains and headaches. Worst of all, I hated it when my brain stopped right in the middle of a sentence. It always rebelled as soon as it figured out that supper was not on its way. Surely God wouldn't ask me to go through all that misery again!

But people in the Bible fasted and prayed when they needed God's help or wisdom. I had to admit that after I had fasted in the past, I was always glad I had done it. Sometimes God would open my eyes to new insights in the Bible. Sometimes He would reveal things He wanted to change in me. Sometimes He'd say yes to a prayer—but then again sometimes He wouldn't. But regardless of what God did or didn't do and what He did or didn't show me, after I fasted, I always ended up a whole lot closer to Him.

For He had made a promise: "I love those who love me; and those who diligently seek me will find me" (Proverbs 8:17).

Yes, in spite of all its misery, fasting always helped me seek God.

That still, small voice, that gentle tug, and now the confirmation of Scripture. I was beginning to get the point. I had to believe this one was from Him.

I'd determined long ago that if He spoke, my answer would be yes. So I headed for the grocery store to buy a bottle of tomato juice. I'd start a three-day juice fast tomorrow.

The first day wasn't all that bad, but day number two was always the worst in a three-day fast for me. It meant I still had another whole day to go, and my stomach already felt like a gnawing cavern. But even then, I had a strange peace in knowing that I was doing what God wanted me to do.

That afternoon I expected the growling in my stomach to get worse. But surprisingly, the longing in my heart had gotten stronger too. I knew exactly how to satisfy my stomach, but I had no idea how to stop that longing. So I cried out, *Lord, I'm so tired of this feeling. Would you please take it away?*

But the longing remained, so I simply moved on and continued my prayers for wisdom for the conference.

By the third day, I was counting the hours. Breakfast was less than a day away! When nighttime fell, I crawled into bed with a hunger in my body and soul. It was time to finish *Gift-Wrapped by God.*

The book was about the gift of sex, its beauty in marriage, and the importance of saving and guarding it until then. I opened it to the final section—a chapter called "Jesus, Your Bridegroom." As I sat in my room and read, a passage of the book caught my attention:

Many women through the centuries have delighted in the intimacy and ecstasy available to every believer with their eternal bridegroom. Madam Guyon, a French woman who lived in the 1600s, experienced a passionate union with Jesus and was imprisoned for her "extreme views." We like this radical lady. She understood the joy of spiritual oneness and encourages us to ask God for this understanding.[2]

Then they quoted Madam Guyon:

"Your spirit is perfectly made to be united with God.... You truly are made to be married to Him. Your spirit can be united to God in this way because that is what it is made

for. Deep and lasting union with God, the spiritual marriage, is what you should ask your Beloved."[3]

A perfect union—a spiritual marriage—what an astonishing
concept! I continued to read to the end of Lorraine and Linda's
next chapter:

> Your bridegroom asks you to love Him totally—with all of
> your being.... Ask the Holy Spirit to breathe on the coals
> of your life and ignite a new flame of passion in you. Tell
> the Spirit that you are not satisfied, that you want more of
> Jesus, that you want to be consumed by Him. Be aban-
> doned in your love for Jesus, and in that abandonment
> something new will stir inside you. You will feel the birth
> of a new passion for Jesus. You will experience the joy of
> Jesus as your bridegroom![4]

I lifted my eyes and pondered that amazing challenge.

For almost five years, I'd been praying that God would help
me experience the depths of His love. I had a personal relationship with Him as well as a certain intimacy. But what I was
experiencing was nothing like what these women were saying was
possible. What I had was only a shadow of what they said God
wanted for me.

Long ago, I heard someone say that the Bible is not a book of
exceptions. It's a book of examples—examples of the relationship
God wants to have with each of us. What I was reading made me
think that this just might be true.

King David had written: "As the deer pants for the water

brooks, so my soul pants for You, O God. My soul thirsts for God, for the living God" (Psalm 42:1–2).

I closed the book, laid it on the nightstand, and thought long and hard about David's words. Did I feel that way about God?

Not really.

I cringed at that admission. That was how I wanted to feel, but something in my relationship with Him was obviously missing—something very special, something I wanted very much.

Madam Guyon told her readers to ask for it. Lorraine and Linda said to ask too. Moses asked God to show him His glory, and sure enough God did.

Yet through the years I had learned that just because I ask for something doesn't mean it will happen. God had made it clear to me that you just can't force His hand. "Our God is in the heavens; He does whatever He pleases" (Psalm 115:3).

Most importantly, who was I to think I could have that kind of intimacy with God? But then again, "You do not have because you do not ask" (James 4:2).

I thought for a moment. *Why not?*

So I covered my face with my hands, bowed my head, and begged my God to give me every bit of Him. I wanted to be as intimate with Him as He would possibly allow. I wanted my spirit united with His. I wanted to know the depths of His love.

I sat in my room and prayed and prayed. I implored Him to show Himself to me. Finally, I reached over, turned out the light, lay down, and continued to plead. If fervor would help my prayers reach His ears, then I would make sure they did.

Nestled in my January blankets, I entreated, beseeched, and begged God to answer. Then, without warning, as if a cloud had

filled the room, I sensed an incredible loving presence. A tender-
ness and peace like I had never known enveloped me, then
melted into every part of my being. The intensity of that presence was not of this world. It was mighty, yet peaceful and
calming.

But the unfathomable perfection of that presence was a brilliant
contrast to all my faults and flaws. Instead of experiencing joy and
delight, I plummeted to a deep sense of unworthiness.

I didn't deserve to experience such love.

All I could see were the things I was not—my limitations, my
weaknesses, things I couldn't do. Even things I didn't like about the
way I looked: my nose, my legs, my feet, my hair... Oh, how I
wanted to be perfect for Him.

Then that silent voice spoke. Its words were filled with love.

*Patti, I know all those things about you. I was the One who made
you that way. And I made you exactly the way I did because that was
what pleased Me most.*

Everything stopped.

I lay motionless as the God of the universe fused the truth of
those words to my soul.

Here I was, in the presence of the One who, in a fleeting
instant, could change anything about me. But even more important, here I was in the presence of the One who *didn't want to.*

I closed my eyes, overwhelmed by that realization. God
designed me just the way He wanted me. He could have given me
a smaller nose, thinner thighs, curly hair. He could have given me
any talent, any attribute He chose. But He made me exactly the
way He did because it pleased Him most.

Oh.

As I lay nestled in those January blankets immersed in that echoing truth, I felt something I'd never felt before—wholly and completely accepted.

Then, drenched in that acceptance, I felt something else I'd never felt before—wholly and completely beautiful.

I grasped the edge of the blankets, held them under my chin, and basked in His love. I delighted in the oneness I sensed with my God. I marveled at the feeling of magnificent beauty born in the eyes of my beholder. Lost in His presence, abiding in His love, soul to Soul, spirit to Spirit.

Then, like the sun on the eastern horizon, a strange anxiety rose up in me. I didn't want to acknowledge it, but I knew I had to be honest. I closed my eyes, lifted my face, and spoke. "God, I know that You want to be this close to everyone. And I know this is selfish, but please don't be this intimate with anyone but me. I want to be special to You."

His response was kind and gentle as He spoke directly to my heart.

Patti, your body is unique. No one will ever have your fingerprints. No one will ever have the same eyes as you. Just as I made your body unique, I made your soul unique too. That is why no one can love Me like you can. You will always be special to Me.

I opened my eyes in amazement and awe of the peace that overcame me. What a piercing Truth! It sliced through the depths of my heart. Then it came to rest, anchored in the harbor of my soul. Now I knew, without a doubt, that out of the billions of people in this world, I was unique and cherished. No one could ever love God like me. In turn, I was amazingly loved and, oh, so amazingly special.

One by one, those teardrops rolled across my temple and onto my pillow. I cried and cried until I fell into a blessed sleep.

The next morning my eyes fluttered open, and I faced the day with a song in my heart. As I flitted around the bed straightening sheets and fluffing pillows, it dawned on me how God had used Lorraine and Linda's conference in my life. I sensed it would go well, but I also sensed that the overarching reason God gave me that opportunity was to lead me to the events of last night. I smiled. But as I began to ponder those events, I began to question. *Could that have happened? Was it really possible?*

But it had to have happened! It was so real—beyond anything I could imagine! I remembered the words, the feeling, the intensity. I'd never experienced anything like it.

Yes, I concluded. It had surely happened. But, of course, I could never tell a soul. People would think I was crazy! Instead, I would treasure that memory in my heart.

My heart…?

Oh my…!

I reached for my chest and drew a breath. My heart felt different—entirely different than it had ever felt before.

It was whole.

The longing was gone, the emptiness filled. Never had I felt so completely satisfied. God had reached into the depths of my heart with a truth that mended its broken places. Then He sealed it with perfect peace, a peace that passes all understanding, a peace that would never fade away.

And it never has.

Since that day three years ago, that emptiness and longing have never returned. The gnawing ache is mercifully gone. That perfect peace remains. My heart is whole, and now I know that I cannot remain silent.

For God wants every one of His children to experience that intimacy with Him. He longs to heal each broken heart and satisfy every soul. His desire is for each of us to abide in the magnificent love of our Bridegroom—the lover for which our souls were made—the only One who will ever make us whole.

I love those who love me;
and those who diligently seek me will find me.

PROVERBS 8:17

p.s.

I sit back amazed as I ponder what God has done to bring this book to completion. I watched Him do miracle after miracle as He led and guided me—sometimes through some pretty rough waters, other times to a place of rest just when I needed it most. He provided everything I needed, not a moment too late or a moment too soon. He opened doors that no man could open and closed doors that would have seemed so simple to walk through. And all just to get me here.

So where is here? It's the same place I've been for an awfully long time—right where He wants me. And what's next? I really don't know for sure, other than it will be the next place He leads and, no doubt, a grand adventure.

But that, my friend, is another story...

note from the author

Patti has developed a free downloadable
Personal Study Guide
to use with
Press Play: Taking the Single Life Off Hold.

This free study guide is designed to help you dig deeper
into Scripture and apply its truths to your own life.
The guide can help you take practical steps
to find your own family,
purpose for living, beauty in the ashes,
and relationship with the Lover of your soul.
You can use the study guide in:
- personal devotions
- small groups
- singles ministries

To download a free Personal Study Guide for
Press Play: Taking the Single Life Off Hold,
visit
www.pattigordon.net.

For more information about Patti Gordon,
or to book Patti to speak at your event or retreat, please visit:
www.pattigordon.net
or e-mail patti@pattigordon.net

notes

1. Oswald Chambers, *My Utmost for His Highest* (Urichsville, OH: Barbour Publishing, 1935), 260.
2. Linda Dillow and Lorraine Pintus, *Gift-Wrapped by God* (Colorado Springs, CO: Waterbrook Press, 2002), 193.
3. Ibid., quoted from Jeanne Guyon, *The Song of the Bride* (Sargent, GA: Seed Sowers Christian Books Publishing House, n.d.), introduction.
4. Ibid., 198–199.